tacos a-z

also by ivy manning

**Weeknight Vegetarian: Simple, Healthy
Meals for Every Night of the Week**

**Instant Pot Family Meals: 60+ Fast,
Flavorful Meals for the Dinner Table**

**Instant Pot Miracle 6 Ingredients
Or Less: 100 No-Fuss Recipes
for Easy Meals Every Day**

**Instant Pot Italian: 100 Irresistible
Recipes Made Easier Than Ever**

**Easy Soups from Scratch with Quick Breads
to Match: 70 Recipes to Pair and Share**

**Better from Scratch: Delicious D.I.Y.
Foods You Can Make at Home**

**Crackers & Dips: More than
50 Handmade Snacks**

**The Adaptable Feast: Satisfying
Meals for the Vegetarians, Vegans,
and Omnivores at Your Table**

**The Farm to Table Cookbook:
The Art of Eating Locally**

a delicious guide to
non-traditional
tacos

tacos a-z

ivy manning

WEST
MARGIN
PRESS

WEST MARGIN PRESS
AN IMPRINT OF TURNER PUBLISHING COMPANY
Nashville, Tennessee
www.turnerpublishing.com

WEST
MARGIN
PRESS

Tacos A to Z: A Delicious Guide to Non-Traditional Tacos

Cover and book design by William Ruoto
Photographs by Dina Avila

Library of Congress Cataloging-in-Publication Data
Names: Manning, Ivy, author.
Title: Tacos A to Z : a delicious guide to non-traditional tacos / Ivy Manning.
   Description: Nashville, Tennessee : West Margin Books, an imprint of Turner
   Publishing Company, [2023] | Includes index.
Identifiers: LCCN 2022057619 (print) | LCCN 2022057620 (ebook) | ISBN
   9781513141428 (hardcover) | ISBN 9781513141435 (paperback) | ISBN
   9781513141442 (epub)
Subjects: LCSH: Tacos. | Cooking, Mexican. | LCGFT: Cookbooks.
Classification: LCC TX836 .M36 2023 (print) | LCC TX836 (ebook) | DDC
   641.84--dc23/eng/20221202
LC record available at https://lccn.loc.gov/2022057619
LC ebook record available at https://lccn.loc.gov/2022057620

Printed in Canada

CONTENTS

CONTENTS

INTRODUCTION

My first restaurant job was in college, at Pasqual's Cantina, a hip Tex-Mex restaurant in Madison, Wisconsin. I was eager to learn but had zero restaurant experience, so I started as a dishwasher. I scrubbed out massive bean pots that nearly outweighed me (that's how you get black bean stains in the armpits of all your T-shirts, by the way), washed dishes, worked until I was giddy, and fell in love with working in a kitchen. After begging for what seemed like an eternity, I was finally allowed to enter the cooking side of the kitchen.

There, I learned how to make salsas, pressure-cook dozens of pounds of chicken, stew beans from scratch, and manage dozens of tortillas at a time on the massive flat-top grill. I was schooled in the endless variety of dishes that could be composed from three kinds of tortillas, five different proteins from pork verde to chorizo, three kinds of beans, two kinds of sauce (green and red), a rainbow of salsas, and special-order tweaks. The sing-song barrage of orders called out in short-hand slang stays with me to this day—"three tacos blue, chicken, yellow chor, flour refry, and a flour faj pinto, no moo!" I was amazed by how many variables there could be in food, and how creative I could be not just in that kitchen, but every kitchen. The combinations of ingredients were endless!

That first restaurant job sparked in me a love of cooking. From culinary school to catering gigs, fine dining restaurant jobs to teaching cooking classes, thirty years later, I owe a lot to that first job. So, when I sat down to write this, my tenth cookbook, it made sense to return to my first kitchen love: tacos.

So, why the A to Z, and why non-traditional tacos? Well, while I have the utmost respect for the time-honored traditions that make Latinx cuisine great, my roots are not Latinx. There are more knowledgeable folks than I to write a book about authentic tacos. But like all genius ideas, tacos—essentially wrapping savory morsels of food in tortillas and eating them out of hand—is an idea that has inspired chefs all over the world to create their own spin on tacos, and I'm one of them. This book will look at tacos through that lens of creativity, approaching tacos as a springboard for meals inspired by cooking from all over the world, from Chiang Mai to Chattanooga. In fact, there are so many ways to fill a taco that when I sat down to organize my thoughts, I found that I could easily cook a taco for every letter of the alphabet! So I did.

INTRODUCTION

In this book I'll show you how to build your own homemade puffy, bendy, delicious corn and flour tortillas with detailed instructions to guide you through the process and convince you that homemade tortillas are worth making from scratch. Then I'll launch into the tacos themselves, the A to the Z: Dorito-coated Avocado Fry Tacos with Sriracha Mayo (page 15) to Za'atar Chicken Tacos (page 101), and everything in between.

While a few tacos in this book have roots in Mexican or Mexican American dishes like Mole Chicken Tacos (page 55) and New Mexican Chile-Dipped Chicken Taquitos (page 59), most recipes will introduce you to taco ideas you've never heard of. Try the English Breakfast Tacos (page 29) for recovering from last night's pub outing, or That '70s Taco (page 81), a cheeky nostalgic take on American crispy-shell ground meat tacos complete with Tater Tots. And don't forget dessert: there's Chocolate-Dipped Ice Cream Tacos (page 21), which is the best thing to happen to ice cream since the sugar cone.

Other recipes in this book are a nod to chefs and cultures that have taken the taco idea and run with it, like the K-Mex invention of Korean Kalbi Tacos (page 49), Hawaiian-style versions like Yellowtail Tacos with Mango-Avocado Salsa (page 99), or upscale restaurant interpretations like Duck Tacos with Orange Ginger Radish Salsa (page 25). For Meatless Monday there's plant-based tacos like satisfying shiitake "bacon"-stuffed Umami Tacos (page 85) and Quinoa and Veggie Double Tacos layered with a crispy taco shelled tucked inside a soft guacamole-smeared flour tortilla—a taco that really delivers on the texture and the flavor front.

Of course, there are tacos I developed simply because they are stuffed with the things I love to eat—crispy Cajun-flavored Oyster Tacos with Celery Root Remoulade (page 63) and umami-rich Hong Kong XO sauce–enhanced XO Shrimp and Cheese Toasty Tacos (page 95), for instance. I've slipped in a bunch of comfort food faves like crispy chicken strips in Buffalo Chicken Tacos with Homemade Ranch Dressing (page 17) and the Royale with Cheese (page 73), which is perfect for burger cravings. There are also spicy food fixes like Vindaloo Pork Tacos (page 87) and Jamaican-inspired Jerk Salmon Tacos (page 45).

And because no one likes a naked taco, there's oodles of cremas, salsas, pickled things, and beans in chapter 3 that will keep your tacos well dressed. There's nothing like opening the fridge and finding a zesty homemade Cilantro Lime Crema (page 113) to inspire your next taco. Ditto for a freezer full of savory black beans or rich bacon-y refried beans.

The unifying factor in this crazy range of taco recipes? They're all wrapped in one kind of tortilla or another and they're written for modern kitchens and busy lives. Oh—and they're all delicious!

If you love tacos, this book is for you. I hope it will keep you engaged and help expand your taco repertoire in new and exciting ways. After all, variety is the spice of Taco Tuesday!

CHAPTER 1

FOUNDATIONS

No taco book (even an non-traditional one) can begin without including recipes for DIY tortillas. Yes, you can buy them in the store. Sometimes I still do, especially since there's been a recent explosion of great, artisan-style tortillas available at markets. (Shout-out to Three Sisters Nixtamal in Portland, Oregon!) That said, making your own anything is rewarding, and everything tastes better from scratch. Homemade tortillas are soft, fresh, and taste so much better than the packaged kind.

Although making your own may feel intimidating, it's really very easy. I've taught countless children in cooking camps how to make homemade tortillas, and if those crazy kids can do it, you can too! As one eager eight-year-old once pointed out to me, it's just like playing with Play-Doh, except it tastes much better.

I've suggested which type of tortilla to use for specific taco recipes, but you do you. There really aren't any bad matches provided everything is homemade!

Homemade Corn Tortillas

MAKES **12** (**6-INCH**) TORTILLAS

To prevent the raw dough from sticking when pressing it into a round, I sandwich the ball of dough in between two sheets of stiff zip-top freezer bag. The plastic also serves as a handy device to flip the somewhat delicate tortilla onto your palm and then onto a hot pan. The plastic sheets can be washed and reused multiple times.

Corn tortillas are often made from fresh masa (available at some Latinx markets) made from corn that has been nixtamalized—treated with a base solution to make the corn more digestible, ground, and mixed with liquid to create a soft dough. Fresh masa is highly perishable, though, so it's more practical for home cooks to make tortillas from masa flour (*masa harina* in Spanish). There are different grinds of masa flour; some are coarser and are made for tamale making, while the masa made for tortillas will clearly state "for tortillas" on the label. I like both Maseca and Bob's Red Mill brand. Since the flour is a magnet for pests, I recommend storing the flour in a zip-top bag in the freezer.

To press homemade corn tortillas, you'll need to pick up an inexpensive tortilla press at a kitchen store, Latinx market, or online. My press is a cast-iron one that has lasted me thirty years so far, but you can also pick up a lighter model made of wood. In a pinch, you can use a glass pie plate, if you don't mind using a little elbow grease to exert pressure on the dough to press it down into the desired thickness.

I learned to make tortillas on a flat-top restaurant grill, but at home I use a two-burner griddle or my big cast-iron pan to create a cooking surface that has a hot zone and a cooler zone. Once the tortillas are cooked, they can be stored in the refrigerator for up to about five days, so I usually make a big batch and use them throughout the week. There are reheating instructions at the end of the recipe.

INGREDIENTS

1½ cups (6½ ounces) masa harina (spoon into the measuring cup and level with a knife)

1 cup plus about 2 tablespoons warm water, divided

INSTRUCTIONS

1.   Combine the masa harina and 1 cup of water in a large bowl. Mix and knead with your hands until the mixture comes together into a soft, pliable, Play-Doh-like dough. It will go from very moist to crumbly as the masa absorbs the water.

2.   Test the dough by breaking off a walnut-sized piece and pressing it between your fingers into a 2-inch disk. If it cracks around the edges, it's still too dry. Return the small wad of dough to the rest of the dough, dip your hand into a bowl of water, and keep kneading and dipping your hand in water until the dough texture is smooth and just a tiny bit sticky, with no cracks when pressed into a disk.

3.   Heat a 2-burner griddle on the stove and set one burner to medium-high heat and the other to medium-low heat. Alternatively, heat a cast-iron skillet over medium-high heat with part of the pan set off center from the heat to create a 2-zone cooking area. Place a clean dish towel or cloth napkin near the stove to hold the cooked tortillas.

4.   Cut a zip-top freezer bag apart to create 2 separate pieces. Pinch off a golf ball–sized piece of dough and put it in between the sheets of the plastic bag and put the plastic-sandwiched dough in the center of a tortilla press (or under a glass pie plate; see headnote). Close the press and push down to flatten the dough into a round. Rotate the tortilla bag setup 90 degrees, close the press again, and press down once more. Don't lean into it; the dough will become too thin, and it will be difficult to peel off the plastic.

5.   Open the press, remove the top sheet of plastic, and flip the tortilla onto your fingers with about half the tortilla hanging off the ends of your fingers. Gently peel the plastic off the second side of the tortilla. Lay the tortilla on the cool side of the preheated pan. Cook until the tortilla looks dry around the edges, about 1 minute. Flip the tortilla onto the hot side of the pan and cook on the second side until it looks dry around the edges, 20 seconds. Flip again back to the first side and cook on the hot side of the griddle/pan, pressing down gently with a spatula or wadded-up napkin to encourage brown spots on the bottom.

6.   If the dough has the right amount of moisture, the tortilla will puff up a bit as it fills with steam. If the tortilla doesn't puff, moisten your hand and squish the remaining dough to add a bit more moisture. Wrap the cooked tortilla in the waiting towel or napkin. The trapped steam will continue to cook the tortilla as it rests. Repeat with the remaining dough to make 12 tortillas. Once you get a rhythm going, you'll be able to pick up the pace. With a little practice, you'll be able to press a tortilla while cooking another one, creating an assembly line.

7. Once you're done pressing and cooking the tortillas, let them stand in the napkin for about 10 minutes. Serve the tortillas immediately, or cool completely and store them in an airtight bag in the refrigerator for up to 5 days.

TACO TIPS

Reheat the tortillas in a dry skillet over medium-high heat until warm and pliable, about 30 seconds per side. Older tortillas are best reheated in the microwave in a plastic bag with a wadded-up moist paper towel on high heat for 1 minute or so. You can also reheat the tortillas over a stovetop steamer pan, wrapped in a clean dish towel until warmed through, 5 minutes.

Homemade Half and Half Tortillas

MAKES **12** (**6-INCH**) TORTILLAS

The masa harina in this recipe gives these tortillas a buttery corn flavor while the gluten in the all-purpose flour gives them a lovely pliability and ease of handling, making them an ideal recipe if you're new to making your own tortillas.

You can press the tortillas in a tortilla maker (see page 3, corn tortillas) or roll out the tortillas between 2 stiff pieces of plastic (such as sheets of zip-top freezer bag) with a rolling pin or press them between sheets of plastic under a glass pie plate; the choice is yours. These tortillas store well; just stash the leftovers in the fridge and they'll go fast. I've included reheating instructions below.

INGREDIENTS

1 cup (4.25 ounces) all-purpose flour (spoon and level)
1 cup (4.25 ounces) masa harina for tortillas (spoon and level)
2 tablespoons vegetable oil, lard, bacon drippings, coconut oil, shortening, or room temperature butter
½ teaspoon salt
⅔ cup warm water, plus more for adjusting

INSTRUCTIONS

1. Put the flour, masa flour, fat, and salt in a medium bowl and stir with your fingers until the fat is well rubbed into the flour, and the mixture looks sandy. Add the water and mix with a wooden spoon until the mixture comes together. Knead in the bowl until smooth, 30 seconds. If the dough feels crumbly, dip your hand in water and continue to knead. The dough should feel like Play-Doh, moist, but with just a hint of

stickiness. Divide the dough into 12 golf ball–sized pieces, roll them into balls, and cover loosely with plastic.

2. Heat a 2-burner griddle over medium-high heat and medium-low heat or heat a cast-iron skillet over medium-high heat with part of the pan set off center to create a 2-zone cooking area. Place a clean dish towel or cloth napkin near the stove to hold the tortillas.

3. Cut a zip-top freezer bag apart to create 2 separate sides. Put one dough ball in between the sheets of the plastic bag and roll a rolling pin over it or press down with a clear pie plate until the dough has formed a round that is approximately 6-inches in diameter.

4. Remove the top sheet of plastic and flip the tortilla into your palm. Peel off the plastic and lay the tortilla on the cool side of the grill. Cook until the tortilla looks dry and opaque white around the edges, about 1 minute. Flip the tortilla onto the hot side of the grill and cook on the second side until it looks dry around the edges, 20 seconds. Flip again back to the first (browned) side and cook on the hot side of the griddle/pan for a few seconds; the tortilla will puff up a bit. Press down gently with the spatula to encourage brown spots on the bottom.

5. Wrap the tortilla in the waiting towel or napkin. The trapped steam will continue to cook the tortilla as it rests. Repeat with the remaining tortillas and let them stand for 5 to 15 minutes. Serve immediately, or cool and store in an airtight bag in the refrigerator for up to 3 days.

TACO TIPS

To reheat the tortillas, put them in a plastic bag, add a wadded-up moist paper towel to the bag, and microwave on high heat for 1 minute. Alternatively, wrap the tortillas in a clean towel and steam them in a steamer over simmering water until warmed, 5 minutes.

Homemade Flour Tortillas

MAKES **8 TO 9 (6-INCH)** TORTILLAS

Once you make homemade flour tortillas and see how easy (and fun) it is, you'll never go back to the stale store-bought tortillas. Adding a bit of fat in whatever form you'd like—butter, coconut oil, olive oil, bacon drippings, lard, ghee—makes the dough exceptionally pliable and easy to work with. The trick is to get the water to flour ratio right, adding water a tablespoon at a time if the dough cracks when you roll it out.

INGREDIENTS

2 cups (8½ ounces) all-purpose flour

¾ teaspoon baking powder

¾ teaspoon salt

3 tablespoons vegetable oil, lard, bacon drippings, coconut oil, shortening, or room temperature butter

⅓ to ½ cup hot water

INSTRUCTIONS

1. Put the flour, baking powder, and salt in a medium bowl and whisk to combine. Add the fat and rub it into the flour with your fingers until the mixture looks like fine pebbles. Add ⅓ cup of water and stir and knead until the dough comes together. Add 1 to 2 tablespoons of water if the dough seems dry.

2. Transfer the dough to a lightly oiled counter and knead until smooth, 1 minute. Cover the dough and let it rest for 10 minutes. Press a small ball of dough into a 3-inch disk with your hands; if the dough develops cracks around the edges and feels dry, knead a little more water into the dough, 1 tablespoon at a time.

3. Divide the dough into 8 balls, about the size of a golf ball. Heat a cast-iron skillet over medium-high heat. Put a clean dish towel next to the stove to keep the tortillas warm as you cook them.

4. Roll dough balls into 6-inch round tortillas (don't get peevish if your tortillas aren't perfectly round as they'll be perfectly delicious, and that's what matters). Cook the tortillas in batches on the hot skillet, occasionally pressing down gently with a wadded-up napkin to make sure they're evenly cooked on the bottom, about 2 minutes. Flip the tortillas and cook on the second side until browned in places, 1 minute. Wrap the tortillas in the towel and repeat with the remaining dough. Serve immediately.

TACO TIPS

The finished dough can be kept in an airtight container for up to 5 days in the fridge; just pinch off what you need to make tortillas on the fly.

A NOTE ABOUT CRISPY TACO SHELLS

I have made homemade crispy taco shells. It's a nifty project, but it requires a lot of finesse, time, and they must be eaten immediately while they're still hot—so they're not convenient for family meals as you can only fry about two at a time.

For these reasons, I recommend using packaged crispy taco shells for the recipes in this book. The secret to making the crispy shells great is to toast them in a 350°F oven until they're warm, about 5 minutes. This quick trip to the oven eradicates any staleness and adds a lovely crunch.

CHAPTER 2

THE ALPHABET OF TACOS

Avocado Fry Tacos with Sriracha Mayo

SERVES **4**

Breading slices of avocado and pan-frying them gives you an incredible textural mouthful: first crispy breading (crushed Cool Ranch Doritos #FTW), then cool, creamy avocado. Do try it, even if you think it sounds odd; avocado fries are absolutely one of the best taco fillings. I mix convenient bagged coleslaw with creamy sweet-spicy homemade Sriracha Mayo, but bottled Sriracha mayonnaise is available too. Be sure to use avocados that are still a little firm; very ripe avocados will fall apart when handled.

INGREDIENTS

½ cup flour

½ teaspoon salt

½ teaspoon pepper

3 eggs

6 cups (about 6 ounces) Cool Ranch Doritos or regular corn tortilla chips

2 large medium-firm avocados

1 cup avocado or safflower oil

3 cups bagged coleslaw shredded cabbage mix

½ cup Sriracha Mayo (page 117)

8 (6-inch) homemade corn or flour tortillas, or packaged tortillas, warmed

1 (2.25-ounce) can sliced California ripe black olives, drained

INSTRUCTIONS

1.   Preheat the oven to 325°F. Put a cooling rack on top of a baking sheet and set aside.

2.   Set up a breading station: Mix the flour, salt, and pepper on a dinner plate. Beat the eggs in a large, shallow bowl. Put the Doritos or corn chips in a plastic bag and use the flat

side of a meat mallet or rolling pin to smash the chips until they are the texture of panko breadcrumbs. Pour the crumbs onto a dinner plate.

3. Cut the avocado in half and gently squeeze the half with the pit until it falls out of the avocado. Use a large serving spoon to gently scoop the avocado halves out of their skins in one piece. Cut the avocado lengthwise into ½- to 1-inch-wide slices.

4. Pour the oil into a large (12-to-14-inch) skillet and heat over medium-high heat until shimmering and a test tortilla chip added to the oil turns golden brown within 4 seconds. While the oil is heating, bread about half of the avocado slices.

5. First, dredge the avocado in the flour mixture, shaking off the excess. Next, dip the slices in the beaten eggs, letting the excess drip back into the bowl. Then place the slices on the plate with the crushed Doritos. Spoon some crumbs over the top of the avocados and press so the slices are coated all over in crumbs.

6. Fry the avocado slices in batches without crowding, carefully flipping them once while cooking, until golden brown, 2 to 3 minutes. Transfer with a slotted spoon or spatula to the prepared cooling rack/baking sheet and keep warm in the oven while frying the remaining avocado slices.

7. Mix the slaw mix with the Sriracha mayo in a small bowl. Put 2 to 3 slices of avocado in each tortilla and top with the slaw and olives. Serve immediately.

TACO TIPS

The avocado fries can be cooked in batches in an air fryer set to 350°F. Mist the avocado fries generously with avocado or olive oil spray and cook for 3 minutes per side.

Buffalo Chicken Tacos with Homemade Ranch Dressing

SERVES **4**

Hot wings are awesome. So is homemade ranch dressing. Put the two together in a taco, and you've got yourself an ideal meal to trot out for your next big game-watching party. Frozen breaded chicken tenders stand in for the bone-in wings here, so it's not exactly authentic "wings," but the flavors—zippy hot wing sauce, cooling salad with celery dressed in creamy ranch dressing—are 100 percent Buffalo.

INGREDIENTS

For the ranch:

¼ cup buttermilk

¼ cup mayonnaise

¼ cup sour cream

1 tablespoon chives

½ teaspoon dried dill

¼ teaspoon garlic powder

¼ teaspoon celery salt

⅛ teaspoon pepper

For the tacos:

24 ounces frozen breaded chicken tenders (such as Tyson Crispy Chicken Strips)

2 cups mixed baby greens

4 celery stalks, thinly sliced

⅓ cup Frank's RedHot Buffalo Wings Hot Sauce, plus more for serving

8 (6-inch) homemade corn tortillas (page 3), flour tortillas (page 9), or store-bought tortillas, warmed

INSTRUCTIONS

1. In a small bowl, whisk together the buttermilk, mayonnaise, sour cream, chives, dill, garlic powder, celery salt, and pepper until smooth. Pour into a squeeze bottle or jar. You will have more than you need; store leftover dressing in the refrigerator for up to a week.

2. Bake or air-fry the chicken tenders according to package instructions; this will take 18 to 20 minutes. While the chicken tenders bake, make the celery salad. Toss the greens and celery with enough of the ranch dressing to lightly coat the leaves.

3. When the chicken strips are ready, roughly chop them (2 to 3 chunks per chicken tender) and drizzle them with the wing sauce. Don't coat the tenders completely; you want to have some areas of the breading left dry to retain their crunch. Fill the tortillas with the salad and tenders and serve with additional dressing and wing sauce at the table for those who want more on their tacos.

TACO TIPS

For a lighter version of this taco, coat 1½ pounds of sliced raw chicken breast with 1 tablespoon safflower oil and season with salt and pepper. Grill over medium-high heat or broil the tenders until just cooked through, about 4 minutes per side. Chop and toss with the wing sauce before proceeding with the recipe.

Chocolate-Dipped Ice Cream Tacos

SERVES 8 TO 10

I love the ice cream novelties that were called Choco Tacos. A genius fusion of a crisp taco-shaped waffle cone stuffed with ice cream, the sweet treat was invented by Alan Drazen, senior VP of the Jack and Jill Ice Cream Company, and later sold to Klondike. Sadly, the tacos were discontinued in August of 2022. Here's my answer to their absence on the market: a recipe for simple home-made crispy cookie shells folded into a taco shape, filled with softened ice cream, and dipped in homemade chocolate candy coating. While the coating is still unset, you can dip the taco in chopped salted peanuts, crushed dehydrated berries, sprinkles, or cinnamon crunch cereal . . . whatever strikes your fancy!

INGREDIENTS

For the taco cookie shells and ice cream:

2 large egg whites

¼ cup light brown sugar, lightly packed

½ teaspoon vanilla extract

½ teaspoon cinnamon

⅛ teaspoon salt

½ cup plus 1 tablespoon (2¾ ounces) all-purpose flour (spoon the flour into the
    measuring cup and level with a knife)

2 tablespoons unsalted butter, melted

6 cups chocolate and vanilla swirl ice cream, softened slightly

For the chocolate coating and toppings:

½ cups (3 ounces) dark chocolate (at least 65 percent), chopped

1½ tablespoons solid coconut oil

1 cup toppings of your choice (see headnote)

INSTRUCTIONS

1. Preheat the oven to 350°F and adjust an oven rack to the center position. Line a rimmed baking sheet with parchment. Using a 4-inch bowl or ramekin, trace 3 circles on the parchment with a pencil. Flip the parchment paper and set aside.

2. Set a 1-inch-thick book with a long spine (something like a picture book works well) up next to the oven and place cans on either side of the book to steady it. You'll use the book as a form to mold the flat cookies into taco shapes as they come out of the oven. Set a dish towel and a rectangular casserole dish on the counter as well.

3. Whisk the egg whites, brown sugar, vanilla, cinnamon, and salt until smooth, breaking up any lumps of brown sugar. Whisk in ½ cup of the flour. Add the butter and whisk until smooth. Add the remaining tablespoon of flour and whisk until smooth.

4. Spoon 1 tablespoon of the batter into the center of each traced circle and spread evenly into 4-inch rounds, using a back-and-forth motion. You may need to steady the parchment with your fingertips as you spread. Put the baking sheet on the center rack of the oven and bake until the rounds are light golden brown on the edges but still pliable, 10 to 12 minutes.

5. Moving quickly, scoop up a cookie with a spatula and set it on the spine of the book. Gently push the cookie down over the spine of the book to create a taco shape; repeat with the other 2 cookies. Put a towel over the cookies (making sure that the cookies are centered on the spine of the book) and hold the cookies down for a few seconds. Let the cookies cool a bit on the book until set, pushing the cookies down a bit if they've sprung back. They will crisp up and retain their folded shape as the dough cools. Hang the cooled cookies on the rim of the casserole dish where they will continue to cool and set.

6. Continue the baking and bending process with the remaining batter to make 8 taco-shaped cookies. (You may be able to make a few more with the batter; I've calculated this recipe to factor in a few that break or crack.)

7. Gently spoon about ⅔ cup of ice cream into a cookie, adding more to fill the taco all the way up to the edges. Smooth with an offset spatula and place the taco upright in the

casserole dish. Repeat with remaining tacos and ice cream. Freeze for at least 1 hour (wrap casserole dish with plastic or foil if freezing for longer than an hour as the ice cream will pick up any off flavors in the freezer).

8. To make the crispy chocolate shell, put the chocolate and coconut oil in a medium microwave-safe bowl. Microwave on high heat for 1 minute. Stir and continue to microwave in 30-second increments, stirring in between, until the mixture is smooth and glossy. (Alternatively, put the chocolate and coconut oil in a heat-proof bowl set over simmering water on the stove and stir until smooth.)

9. Dip the top edges of the tacos in the chocolate and then very quickly dip the chocolate-covered part of the taco in your choice of toppings. Let the tacos stand at room temperature until the chocolate solidifies into a hard coating, about 2 minutes. Enjoy now, or store in the freezer in a covered container for up to 3 weeks.

TACO TIPS

Traditional store-brand ice creams, as opposed to gourmet brands, work best for this recipe. They have a fair amount of air whipped into them, which makes it easier to spread evenly into the taco shells.

Duck Tacos with Orange Ginger Radish Salsa and Chili Crisp

SERVES 4 (MAKES 8 TACOS)

If you're a little nervous about cooking duck, don't be! With this foolproof trick of browning duck breasts slowly on the stove and then finishing them in the oven, you'll always arrive at exceptionally juicy meat and a delicious, crispy golden skin. All the better to tuck into a taco and pair with an orange ginger salsa!

I add generous drizzles of chili crisp on top of these tacos—not that the tacos really need it; I'm just hooked! The Sichuan condiment of dried chilies, black beans, garlic, and oil adds a little more heat, crunchiness, and lots more umami (I'm an S&B brand fan but Fly by Jing and Mr. Bing are also great brands to try).

INGREDIENTS

For the duck breast:

3 (7-ounce) boneless, skin-on duck breasts

2½ teaspoons kosher salt

Zest of 1 large orange (about 1½ tablespoons)

2 teaspoons finely grated fresh ginger

1½ teaspoons five-spice powder

½ teaspoon freshly ground black pepper

8 (6-inch) packaged blue corn tortillas, warmed (or homemade corn tortillas, page 3)

¼ cup chili crisp condiment

For the orange ginger radish salsa:

4 navel oranges

4 radishes, grated

3 green onions, thinly sliced

1 serrano chile pepper, finely chopped

2 teaspoons finely grated ginger

Salt to taste

INSTRUCTIONS

1. Preheat oven to 425°F. Score the duck breast skin with a sharp knife to make a crisscross pattern. Rub the duck all over with the salt, orange zest, ginger, spices, and pepper. Marinate for at least 30 minutes at room temperature or in the refrigerator for up to 4 hours.

2. While the duck is marinating, make the salsa. Cut the top and bottom off the oranges and trim away any white pith on the outside of the oranges with a sharp paring knife. Cut each orange into segments by using the paring knife to cut the orange flesh away from the translucent membranes that separate them. Chop the orange segments into small pieces. Combine in a medium, non-reactive bowl with the radishes, green onions, serrano chile, ginger, and salt to taste. Set aside at room temperature.

3. Heat a large ovenproof sauté pan or cast-iron skillet over medium heat until warm. Place the duck skin side down in the dry pan, reduce to medium-low heat, and cook until the duck fat under the skin has rendered off and the skin is crisp and golden brown, 15 to 20 minutes.

4. Flip the duck breasts and place the pan in the oven. Bake until an instant-read thermometer registers 135°F when inserted into the thickest part of the meat, 5 to 8 minutes. (The meat will be rosy pink when sliced.) Transfer the duck breasts to a cutting board and allow them to rest for 10 minutes.

5. Slice the duck breasts very thinly at a 45-degree angle with a sharp carving knife. Add the sliced duck to the tortillas and top with forkfuls of the orange salsa, letting excess orange juices fall back into the bowl. Dab each taco with the chili crisp condiment and serve.

TACO TIPS

Use a very sharp carving knife and a sawing motion to get through the skin when preparing the duck breasts. Not only does this encourage the marinade to infuse the meat with flavor, but it also helps the fat melt for maximum crispiness.

Don't throw out the flavorful drippings in the sauté pan! Pour them off into a small bowl and reserve them for the best fried rice you will ever have.

English Breakfast Tacos

SERVES 4 (MAKES 4 LARGE TACOS)

The "full English" breakfast is a huge plate including eggs, sauteed mushrooms, charred tomatoes, sausages, and barbecue beans—the perfect cure for the aftereffects of a night out at the pub. It's easy to throw together, folds messily into a flour tortilla, and will cure what ails you. Substitute vegetarian sausages for pork ones, if you like.

INGREDIENTS

1 can cannellini or great northern beans, rinsed and drained

¼ cup HP Sauce (or your favorite steak sauce)

¼ cup ketchup

1 tablespoon brown sugar

2 tablespoons olive oil

8 ounces cremini mushrooms, thickly sliced

1 teaspoon salt, divided

8 heat-and-serve pork, chicken, or vegetarian breakfast sausages

2 pinches granulated garlic powder

1 cup cherry tomatoes, halved

1 tablespoon butter

6 large eggs, beaten

¼ teaspoon black pepper

1 cup grated English Cheddar cheese (or other sharp Cheddar)

4 (6-to-8-inch) flour tortillas, warm

INSTRUCTIONS

1. Combine the beans, HP Sauce, ketchup, and brown sugar in a small saucepan and bring to a simmer over medium heat. Cook, stirring occasionally, until the mixture has thickened slightly, and the flavors have married, 10 minutes. Keep warm, uncovered, over low heat.

2. In a large nonstick skillet, heat the oil over medium-high heat. When the oil is hot, add the mushrooms and 1 pinch of salt to the pan. Add the sausages to the other side of the pan and cook, stirring occasionally with a rubber spatula, until the mushrooms have given off their liquid and are well browned and the sausages are heated through, about 5 minutes. Add the garlic powder to the mushrooms and transfer everything to a bowl, cover, and set aside.

3. Return the skillet to medium-high heat. Add the cherry tomatoes and cook, stirring occasionally, until they begin to brown and collapse, 3 minutes. Transfer to a bowl, cover, and set aside.

4. Return the pan to medium heat. Add the butter and swirl to coat the bottom of the pan. Add the eggs and sprinkle with ½ teaspoon salt and the pepper. Cook, stirring constantly with a rubber spatula, until curds just begin to form, about 5 seconds. Swirl the pan as you stir to encourage the uncooked egg to settle evenly in the bottom of the pan. Reduce heat to low, sprinkle the cheese over the eggs, and cover with a lid and continue to cook until the top is set but still a little creamy, 1 to 2 minutes more.

5. Pile the eggs, beans, sausages, and mushrooms into the tortillas. Spoon the cherry tomatoes over the tacos and serve immediately.

TACO TIPS

If you're a fan of the English version of Heinz baked beans and like them, substitute them for the homemade beans for a more authentic experience.

Fish and Chips Tacos with Pea Guacamole

SERVES 4 (MAKES 8 TACOS)

If you've ever visited the UK, you know the joys of going to a "chippy" to get crispy fried fish and chips wrapped up in a newspaper cone. They're a lovely walk-and-nibble meal. So why not wrap the fish in a warm flour tortilla? Pan-seared fish and fries make this a quick weeknight win. The traditional side dish for fish and chips is "mushy peas," which are delicious when blended with mashed avocado, mint, and a squeeze of lemon.

INGREDIENTS

For the pea guacamole:

½ cup frozen peas, defrosted

1 large, ripe avocado, halved and pitted

2 tablespoons chopped fresh mint

1 tablespoon lemon juice

1 pinch cayenne pepper

Salt, for seasoning

For the fish and chips tacos:

4 cups (8 ounces) frozen French fries

1¼ pounds cod, halibut, or other sustainable white fish fillet

1 tablespoon Taco Seasoning (page 81, That '70s Taco)

1¼ teaspoons salt, plus more for seasoning

2 tablespoons safflower oil

8 warm flour tortillas

2 cups finely shredded green cabbage

Malt vinegar or lemon wedges, for serving

INSTRUCTIONS

1. For the guacamole, combine the peas, avocado, mint, lemon juice, and cayenne pepper in a food processor and pulse until smooth. Spoon into a bowl and season with salt to taste. Cover and set aside.

2. Preheat the oven and prepare the fries according to package instructions, or use an air fryer to cook them, if desired. Err on the side of well done; you want the fries to be crispy, so they will hold up against the moisture from the fish and guacamole.

3. Meanwhile, cut the fish into chunky strips, about ½ to ¾ inches wide. Sprinkle them with the taco seasoning and salt. Heat the oil in a large nonstick pan or cast-iron skillet over high heat until almost smoking. Add the fish strips, reduce heat to medium, and cook until they are cooked through (they will be opaque white throughout), about 2½ minutes per side.

4. Spread the guacamole on the tortillas. Divide the fries and fish among the tortillas, top with the cabbage and serve with malt vinegar or lemon on the side for splashing/squeezing on the tacos.

TACO TIPS

Are you a purist who needs a quick fried fish fix? Substitute frozen fish fingers (I like Gorton's Crunchy Fish Sticks) for the seared fish. Cook according to package instructions.

Greek-Style Lamb Tacos

SERVES **4** (MAKES **8** TACOS)

Take the fresh flavors of Greek gyros—lamb, garlic, fresh dill, oregano, fresh tomatoes, creamy yogurt sauce—and substitute the pita with puffy skillet-cooked flour tortillas and you've got a gyro-barbacoa taco mash-up made in heaven. Buy a boneless leg of lamb roast and discard the netting used to tie it or ask your butcher to butterfly the leg for you for this recipe. Since most leg of lamb roasts are at least 3 pounds, you'll have delicious leftovers, which can be reheated and used for more tacos or the best Greek salad you'll ever have (see Taco Tips below for how to reheat).

INGREDIENTS

For the lamb:
1 (3-pound) butterflied boneless leg of lamb
¼ cup olive oil
¼ cup red wine vinegar
4 teaspoons dried oregano
1 tablespoon cumin seeds
1 tablespoon granulated garlic powder
1½ teaspoons salt
1 teaspoon black pepper

For the tzatziki:
1 cup plain Greek yogurt
½ cup seeded, finely chopped cucumber
2 teaspoons finely chopped jalapeno chile pepper (seeds discarded, if desired)
½ teaspoon finely chopped garlic, smashed with the side of a knife into a paste
A few pinches salt

For the tacos:

2 cups shredded romaine lettuce

1 large tomato, chopped

½ cup roughly chopped fresh dill

¼ cup chopped red onion

8 (6-inch) homemade flour tortillas (page 9), or store-bought tortillas, warmed

INSTRUCTIONS

1. Remove the netting or string from the roast if present. Combine the olive oil, vinegar, oregano, cumin, garlic powder, salt, and pepper and rub all over the lamb, including on the inside of the roast, where the bone has been removed. Place in a non-reactive container or large zip-top bag and marinate in the refrigerator for at least 1½ hours and up to 24 hours.

2. Combine the yogurt, cucumber, jalapeno, and garlic in a small bowl. Season with salt to taste, cover, and set aside at room temperature.

3. Preheat a gas or charcoal grill over medium-high heat with a cool zone (a grill thermometer should read about 375°F). Remove the lamb from the marinade and shake off the excess. Place the lamb over the hot part of the grill fat side down, spread out but arranged so that all the sections are touching to create a compact, even mound on the grill. Grill uncovered until well browned on the outside, about 3 minutes per side. Watch carefully and flick the grill with cold water if there are any flare-ups.

4. Transfer the lamb to the cool zone and grill, covered, until an instant-read thermometer registers 140°F, 30 to 40 minutes. Transfer to a cutting board, cover with foil, and let the meat rest for 10 minutes before carving it into thin slices.

5. Meanwhile, put the lettuce, tomato, dill, and onion in a medium bowl and toss to combine. Divide the lamb among the tortillas. Top with tzatziki and lettuce mixture. Serve immediately.

6. Store leftovers, with remaining juices left on the cutting board, in an airtight container in the refrigerator for up to 5 days.

TACO TIPS

To reheat leftovers, arrange the lamb slices on a foil-lined baking sheet, brush or spray with olive oil, and broil on the top rack of the oven until crispy on the edges, 1 to 2 minutes.

Hawaiian Grilled Chicken Tacos with Spicy Pineapple Salsa

SERVES 4 (MAKES 8 TACOS)

Sweet and spicy, that's the thing. This pineapple-soy Hawaiian-style marinade makes the grilled chicken extra tender by breaking down the proteins in the meat while infusing it with rich, gingery flavor. The salsa features fresh pineapple, and grilling it intensifies its tropical flavor, while grilling poblano chiles and sweet onion amps up the sweetness and earthiness. I love these tacos all by themselves, but you could also serve them with generous sprinkles of Cotija cheese to add a salty counterpoint, if you are so inclined.

INGREDIENTS

For the tacos:

6 boneless, skinless chicken thighs (about 2 pounds)

½ cup pineapple juice or mirin

¼ cup soy sauce

4 teaspoons finely grated fresh ginger

1 tablespoon finely chopped garlic

2 teaspoons toasted sesame oil

8 (6-inch) corn or flour tortillas, warmed

2 cups finely shredded red cabbage or Pickled Red Cabbage (page 119)

For the salsa:

3 thick (1-inch) slices of fresh pineapple, trimmed

1 thick (1-inch) slice Maui onion

1 poblano chile pepper, quartered lengthwise, seeds and core discarded

1 tablespoon safflower oil

5 medium garlic cloves, papery outer skins discarded but cloves left in their innermost
   skins
1 tablespoon lime juice
1 teaspoon sriracha
Salt to taste

INSTRUCTIONS

1. Combine the chicken, pineapple juice, soy sauce, ginger, garlic, and sesame soil in a small non-reactive container and let the chicken marinate at room temperature for at least 30 minutes, but ideally in the refrigerator for 24 hours.

2. Preheat a clean, well-oiled gas grill, charcoal grill, or grill pan over medium-high heat. Brush the pineapple, onion (see Taco Tips), and pepper with the safflower oil and place them on the grill. Put the garlic on the grill as well (see Taco Tips). Grill uncovered, flipping the ingredients once, pressing down on the peppers with a spatula to char the skin, until everything is charred but still has some texture, about 10 minutes total.

3. Transfer the salsa ingredients to a cutting board. Squeeze the garlic out of the skins. Scrape the charred skin off the pepper and discard (don't be too worried about any skin that won't peel away easily). Cut the hard core away from the pineapple slices and discard. Chop the pineapple, garlic, pepper, and onion and transfer to a bowl. Add the lime juice, sriracha, and salt and stir to combine. Set aside at room temperature.

4. Remove the chicken from the marinade. Pour the marinade in a small saucepan and bring to a boil over medium-high heat; set aside. Put the chicken on the grill and grill uncovered, turning once, until the chicken is no longer pink in the center or an instant-read thermometer registers 170°F when inserted into the thickest part of the thighs, 8 to 15 minutes, depending on the size of the pieces. Brush the chicken frequently with the boiled marinade during the last 3 minutes of cooking.

5.   Transfer the chicken to a cutting board and chop it up into bite-size pieces. Divide the chicken and salsa among the tortillas and top with the red cabbage.

TACO TIPS

To prevent the onions and garlic from falling between the grates of outdoor grills, push them onto metal skewers, running the skewers horizontally through all the rings of the onion.

Irish Nachos Tacos

SERVES **4** (MAKES **8** TACOS)

Being Irish American and a third owner of an Irish-themed pub, the concept of Irish nachos has always been a bit of a head-scratcher to me—I've definitely never seen them in Ireland on our family's beverage research trips and it's not on the menu at our pub. That said, there's no denying that this bar food staple is delicious. If you're new to the concept, imagine crispy, zesty roasted potato coins topped with bacon, cheddar cheese, sour cream, and fresh pico de gallo. Tuck that into a taco and you've got a thrifty, tasty meal you can make with ingredients you probably already have on hand and which goes brilliantly with a pint of Smithwick's. Sláinte!

INGREDIENTS

1½ pounds small Yukon Gold potatoes, cut into ¼-inch-thick rounds

2 tablespoons olive oil

2 tablespoons Tajin seasoning (see Taco Tips)

8 (6-inch) homemade flour tortillas (page 9), or store-bought tortillas, warmed

8 strips bacon, cooked and crumbled

1 cup grated Cheddar cheese

1 cup homemade pico de gallo (page 106), or store-bought salsa

¾ cup sour cream

¼ cup chopped pickled jalapeno peppers

2 green onions, thinly sliced

INSTRUCTIONS

1. Place a rimmed baking sheet on the center rack of the oven and preheat the oven to 425°F. (Preheating the baking sheet keeps the potatoes from sticking to the pan.)

2. Toss the potato slices with the olive oil and Tajin seasoning in a large bowl. Open the oven door and quickly pour the potatoes onto the hot pan. Shake the pan vigorously to spread the potatoes out in an even layer. Roast, stirring once, until the potatoes are golden brown, and the thinnest slices are crisp, 25 to 30 minutes.

3. Divide the potatoes among the tortillas. Top with the bacon and cheese. Spoon the pico de gallo over the potato mixture, add a few dollops of sour cream, and sprinkle with pickled jalapenos and green onions. Serve immediately.

TACO TIPS

Tajin is a mildly spicy seasoning mix that is made of red chilies, salt, and crystallized lime that was born in Mexico but is now thankfully available in thirty countries. Look for it in supermarkets in either the produce section or in the seasoning aisle.

Jerk Salmon Tacos

This salmon recipe is inspired by the spicy marinated jerk chicken my chef nephew Alex Jones makes with his wife, Shackai, when she's homesick for Jamaica. I've adjusted the chile heat a tad to better suit the fish (and my wimpy heat tolerance), but the resulting fish still packs a nice wave of fruity heat, sweetness from brown sugar, and earthiness from ginger, allspice, nutmeg, and mace. Paired with a quick, sweet-sour onion, carrot, and bell pepper sauté, these tacos are a lovely way to enjoy grilled or broiled fish.

INGREDIENTS

For the jerk sauce:

½ cup ketchup

3 tablespoons water

2 chopped green onions

2 tablespoons olive oil

1 tablespoon soy sauce

Zest and juice of ½ lime

½ to 1 habanero chile, stemmed, chopped with seeds

2 teaspoons brown sugar

2 teaspoons chopped fresh thyme

1½ teaspoons finely chopped fresh ginger

1 teaspoon chopped garlic

¾ teaspoon ground allspice

¼ teaspoon nutmeg

¼ teaspoon mace

For the tacos:

1½ pounds wild salmon fillet, skin-on, pin bones removed

1 tablespoon olive oil

1 small, sweet onion, thinly sliced

1 red bell pepper, seeded and thinly sliced

1 large carrot, julienned (I use a nifty julienne peeler for this)

2 teaspoons chopped fresh thyme

½ teaspoon salt

2 tablespoons white wine vinegar

1 green onion, chopped

8 (6-inch) homemade corn tortillas (page 3), or store-bought tortillas,
  warmed

INSTRUCTIONS

1. Combine the jerk marinade ingredients in a blender and blend until smooth. Pour half of the sauce over the salmon and set aside at room temperature for 30 minutes. Pour the other half of the sauce in a small saucepan and bring to a simmer over medium-low heat, stirring frequently, until bubbly. Cover and keep warm.

2. Preheat a gas or charcoal grill over medium-high heat or preheat a broiler on high and place an oven rack in the highest position (about 4 inches from the broiler element). Spray a piece of foil with cooking spray.

3. Place the salmon fillet(s) skin side down on the foil and place the foil on the grill. Cover and grill until the fish is cooked through, 10 to 12 minutes. To broil, set the fish on the foil on a baking sheet and broil, rotating the baking sheet once, until the fish is done. (To test for doneness, insert a paring knife in the center of the largest fillet portion and count to three. Carefully touch the dull side of the knife to your bottom lip; it will come out hot when the fish is completely cooked.)

4. While the fish is cooking, make the topping. Heat the olive oil in a large sauté pan over medium-high heat. Add the onion, red bell pepper, carrot, thyme, and salt and sauté until crisp-tender, 4 minutes. Add the vinegar and cook, stirring occasionally, until the vegetables are tender, 3 minutes. Stir in the green onion.

5. Slide a thin-bladed spatula between the salmon skin and the flesh; discard skin. Cut the salmon into 8 equal-sized portions and divide among the tortillas. Top with the sautéed vegetables and serve with the warm jerk sauce on the side.

TACO TIPS

The marinade can also be used on other types of firm fish, chicken, and pork. Increase the marination time to at least 1 hour and up to overnight in the refrigerator if you're going to use meat in lieu of fish.

Korean Kalbi Tacos

SERVES 4 (MAKES 8 TACOS)

These spicy fusion tacos are inspired by chef Eric Silverstein's book, *The Peached Tortilla*. Eric makes genius combinations of Asian and Tex-Mex ingredients for adoring crowds at his restaurants and food carts in Austin, Texas. I adapted his recipe for Korean braised short ribs, shredding them at the end and folding them into hot tortillas with a garnish of Napa cabbage kimchi and sriracha aioli. It's spicy umami meat candy you'll never forget.

INGREDIENTS

3½ pounds bone-in English-cut beef short ribs

1 tablespoon five-spice powder

½ teaspoon salt

½ teaspoon pepper

1 tablespoon safflower oil

1 yellow onion, sliced

6 garlic cloves, peeled and left whole

1 cup low-sodium soy sauce

½ cup mild gochujang paste (Korean red pepper paste)

½ cup rice wine vinegar

½ cup brown sugar, lightly packed

8 (6-inch) homemade corn tortillas (page 3), or store-bought tortillas, warmed

½ cup chopped Napa cabbage kimchi

½ cup cilantro leaves, loosely packed

½ cup Sriracha Mayo (page 117)

INSTRUCTIONS

1. Preheat the oven to 275°F. Rub the short ribs all over with the five-spice powder, salt, and pepper. Heat the oil in a large (4- to 5-quart) Dutch oven over medium-high heat. Sear the short ribs, until they are deeply browned. Do not overcrowd the meat; you may need to work in batches. Transfer to a plate.

2. Reduce the heat to medium, add the onion and garlic, and cook until the onions become limp and begin to brown, 5 minutes. Meanwhile, whisk together the soy sauce, gochujang paste, rice wine vinegar, and brown sugar; set aside.

3. Return the short ribs to the pan meaty side down. Pour the soy sauce mixture over the short ribs and turn with tongs to coat. Add enough water to come halfway up the sides of the short ribs (about ½ to 1 cup), if necessary. Cover with a tight-fitting lid and bake for 1½ hours. Turn the short ribs with tongs and add more water if the pan looks dry. Cover and continue to cook until the meat is very tender (a fork will twist easily when plunged into the meat), 1½ to 2 hours more.

4. Transfer the ribs to a plate with a slotted spoon. Pour the cooking liquid into a gravy separator or large (4-cup) glass measuring cup. Skim off the liquid fat and discard. Shred the meat with 2 forks, discarding bone and connective tissue. Spoon ½ cup of the cooking liquid over the meat. Divide the meat among the tortillas evenly and top with the kimchi and cilantro. Drizzle with the sriracha mayo and serve.

TACO TIPS

To make the short ribs in a slow cooker, sear the recipe as directed, using a large skillet or sauté pan instead of the Dutch oven. Transfer to a slow cooker and add ½ cup of water. Cook on low heat for 7 to 8 hours, or until the meat is very tender.

You can substitute a 3-pound chuck roast for the short ribs if you like. Cut the roast into 4 even pieces and proceed with the recipe.

Linguica, Kale, and Potato Tacos

SERVES 4 (MAKES 8 TACOS)

Linguica is a truly delicious, slightly spicy Portuguese smoked pork sausage that's made with garlic, chilies and/or paprika. My favorite linguica dish is *caldo verde*, a thick Portuguese soup made with linguica (or chouriço), potatoes, and leafy greens. Much more than a sum of its parts, the combo is sublime as a taco filling too. All you need is a few spoonfuls of Roasted Tomato Jalapeno Salsa (page 110) and a sprinkle of queso fresco cheese and you're in taco heaven!

INGREDIENTS

1 tablespoon olive oil

12 ounces linguica sausage, cut into ¼-inch-thick slices

½ large white onion, thinly sliced through root end

1 large (12-ounce) russet potato, peeled, quartered, and thinly sliced

1 pinch salt

½ cup chicken stock

4 cups baby kale or chopped lacinato kale (large ribs removed)

8 (6-inch) homemade corn tortillas (page 3), or store-bought tortillas, warmed

½ cup Roasted Tomato Jalapeno Salsa (page 110)

1 cup crumbled queso fresco or mild feta cheese

INSTRUCTIONS

1. Heat the oil in a large sauté pan over medium-high heat. Add the sausage and cook until browned, 4 minutes. Transfer to a bowl with a slotted spoon, cover, and set aside. Leave the drippings in the pan.

2. Add the onion and potato to the pan, sprinkle with the salt, and reduce heat to medium. Cook, stirring occasionally with a spatula, until the potatoes are lightly browned and nearly tender, 5 minutes. Add the stock, cover, and simmer until the potatoes are tender when pierced with a fork, 5 minutes.

3. Stir in the sausage and kale, and cook uncovered, stirring frequently and breaking up any large slices of potato, until the kale is wilted, 2 minutes. Divide the filling among the tortillas, spoon over the salsa, and sprinkle with the cheese. Serve immediately.

TACO TIPS

Look for Portuguese linguica at well-stocked markets. I like the Silva brand, though it's worth checking out the Hawaiian linguica brands as well. You can also substitute another spicy, smoked sausage such as Boar's Head chicken chorizo sausages, Zenner's chorizo, or Johnsonville's New Orleans andouille. It won't be quite the same, but it'll still be tasty.

Mole Chicken Tacos

A little spicy, sweet, nutty, with just a hint of dark chocolate, mole poblano is an irresistibly complex sauce from the Mexican state of Puebla. Though there's plenty of controversy over the origins of the dish, it has its roots in Aztec culture. Making it is an art—with over 20 ingredients and a long list of steps including toasting chilies, grinding nuts and spices, and long simmering, it's often made especially for festivals and celebrations.

My love of mole poblano has inspired me to create my own (non-traditional) mole version that is much quicker to make. The flavor isn't as complex as traditional mole poblano, but this streamlined recipe is definitely tasty and it satisfies my craving. Note that this recipe makes more than enough sauce for tacos. The leftover sauce freezes well, so I often bank the leftover sauce in the freezer and label it "mole starter" and use it for future dinners—either more chicken tacos or a batch of chili con carne.

INGREDIENTS

1 tablespoon olive oil

1 large white onion (about 2 cups), chopped, divided

1 poblano chile pepper, seeded and chopped

1 tablespoon finely chopped garlic

2 teaspoons ground cumin

1½ teaspoons ground coriander

1½ teaspoons chili powder

½ teaspoon ground cinnamon

½ teaspoon salt

1 (14.5-ounce) can fire-roasted crushed tomatoes with green chilies with juice

½ cup chicken stock

2 tablespoons canned chipotle chilies, chopped

2½ pounds boneless, skinless chicken thighs

1 ounce dark (72% cocoa solids) chocolate, broken into small pieces

1 tablespoon tahini or peanut butter

8 (6-inch) homemade corn tortillas (page 3), or store-bought tortillas, warmed

½ cup crumbled Cotija or feta cheese

⅓ cup chopped cilantro

5 radishes, thinly sliced

INSTRUCTIONS

1. In a large sauté pan, heat the oil over medium heat. When the oil is shimmering, add 1¾ cups of the onion and the poblano chile and sauté until the onion is tender and translucent, 5 minutes. Add the garlic, cumin, coriander, chili powder, cinnamon, and salt and cook, stirring frequently, until fragrant but not browned, 30 seconds.

2. Add the tomatoes, stock, and chipotle chilies and stir to combine. Add the chicken, bring to a simmer, cover, and reduce heat to low. Simmer gently until the chicken is cooked through and tender, 30 minutes. Transfer the chicken to a cutting board and chop; set aside.

3. Remove from heat and add the chocolate and tahini to the sauce. Blend with an immersion blender until smooth. Be very careful; the hot mixture will splash around a bit as it's blended. Alternatively, blend the sauce in a blender with the lid ajar. Return the chicken to the pan and return the sauce to a simmer over medium heat.

4. Serve the chicken in tortillas, topped with the remaining ¼ cup of onions, cheese, cilantro, and radishes. Serve immediately.

TACO TIPS

This recipe can be made in a slow cooker. Sauté the onion, chile, garlic, and spices as directed. Add these to a 6-quart slow cooker along with the chicken and tomatoes. Delete the broth. Cook on low for 8 hours. Proceed with the recipe as directed.

New Mexican Chile-Dipped Chicken Taquitos

SERVES 4 (MAKES 12 TAQUITOS)

Taquitos, or "little tacos" in Spanish, are corn tortilla cylinders tightly rolled around fillings such as shredded meat, and deep-fried (or baked). Mixing shredded chicken with plenty of cheese and a bit of green chilies helps to moisten this filling and keeps it from falling out of the rolls.

I serve these crunchy little tacos with my quick New Mexican red chile sauce for dipping. It's easy to throw together, uses ingredients I always have in my pantry, and it's a crowd-pleasing mix of spicy, earthy, and just a touch sweet. Look for genuine ground New Mexican chilies (not to be confused with "chili powder," which is a blend of spices and herbs used for chili soup) in well-stocked markets or online. I love Los Chileros Chimayo Blend New Mexico Red Chile, but you can also find budget-friendly packets of ground New Mexican chile powder in large supermarkets where Mexican foods are stocked.

INGREDIENTS

For the New Mexican chile dip:

2 tablespoons olive oil

½ cup finely chopped yellow onion

1 tablespoon chopped garlic

2 tablespoons New Mexican chile pepper powder (see Taco Tips)

2½ teaspoons all-purpose flour

½ teaspoon ground cumin

¼ teaspoon oregano (preferably Mexican oregano)

1 pinch cinnamon

1 cup canned tomato sauce

¾ cup chicken stock

1 tablespoon honey

Salt to taste

For the taquitos:

3 cups boneless, skinless, shredded rotisserie chicken (from about ½ a chicken)

1 cup shredded Monterey Jack cheese

1 (4-ounce) can chopped Hatch green chilies, drained

12 (6-inch) homemade corn tortillas (page 3), or store-bought tortillas

2 tablespoons olive oil

INSTRUCTIONS

1. Make the New Mexican chile sauce. Heat the oil in a large saucepan over medium heat. Add the onions and sauté, stirring occasionally, until translucent, 8 minutes. Add the garlic, chile powder, flour, cumin, oregano, and cinnamon and cook, stirring constantly, for 1 minute. Whisk in the tomato sauce, stock, and honey. Reduce heat to low and cook, stirring occasionally, until the flavors have melded, 20 minutes. Season with salt to taste.

2. Meanwhile, make the taquitos. Preheat the oven to 425°F. Line a baking sheet with foil, spray with cooking spray, and set aside. Mix the chicken, cheese, and green chilies in a medium bowl, stirring with a spoon so that the ingredients are evenly blended; set aside.

3. Place the tortillas on a plate and wrap them in a few damp paper towels. Microwave on high until the tortillas are soft and pliable, 1 minute. Spoon about ¼ cup of the chicken mixture in the center of a tortilla in a line running parallel to you (keep remaining tortillas covered with damp paper towels). Roll up the tortilla into a tight cylinder and place seam side down on the prepared baking sheet. Repeat with remaining tortillas and filling, lining up the taquitos so that they are close together but not touching. Brush the taquitos generously with the oil.

4. Bake until the taquitos are crisp and browned on the edges, 15 to 20 minutes. Serve with the New Mexican chile sauce for dipping.

TACO TIPS

You can make this recipe with beans in place of the chicken; see recipes for A Batch of Really Good Black Beans (page 123) or Refried Pinto Beans (page 121).

Oyster Tacos with Celery Root Remoulade

Tacos stuffed with hot, crispy fried oysters topped with a creamy celery root slaw called "remoulade" are a luxury worth having. Par-cooking the oysters for a few seconds in boiling water firms them up just a bit so the oysters won't have even a hint of sliminess, an issue some folks may have with cooked oysters. A simple coating of panko plus Cajun seasoning and a quick, shallow fry makes these oysters supremely crispy while still maintaining their delicious sea flavor.

Celery root lends a mellow celery-like flavor and satisfying crunch to the slaw here, but if you can't find the knobby veg (it looks a bit like a dirty softball with mini celery growing out of the top), substitute bagged coleslaw veggies. To gild the lily just a little, I sprinkle a fistful of fried jalapeno chips (available where bagged fried wonton strips and croutons are sold) on top.

INGREDIENTS

For the remoulade:

½ cup mayonnaise

2 tablespoons grainy mustard

2 tablespoons finely chopped dill pickle

1 green onion, finely chopped

2 teaspoons white wine vinegar

2 teaspoons tomato paste

1 small garlic clove, finely chopped and mashed to a paste

½ teaspoon lemon juice

1 medium (1-pound) celery root (tough outer skin trimmed away), julienned or grated, or ½ bag (4-ounces) coleslaw mix

For the tacos:

1 (16-ounce) jar small or medium shucked raw oysters

Boiling water

½ cup all-purpose flour

½ teaspoon salt

¼ teaspoon pepper

1 large egg

1 cup panko breading

2 tablespoons Cajun seasoning

Safflower oil, for frying

8 homemade corn tortillas (page 3), or store-bought tortillas, warmed

½ cup fried jalapeno chips (see headnote)

INSTRUCTIONS

1. In a medium bowl, whisk the mayonnaise, mustard, dill pickle, green onion, vinegar, tomato paste, garlic, and lemon juice together. Stir in the celery root, cover, and set aside.

2. Rinse the oysters gently in a fine mesh sieve and place them in a heat-proof bowl. Add enough boiling water to just cover the oysters. Count to 15 and then drain the oysters in the fine mesh sieve again. Gently pat the oysters dry with paper towels.

3. Combine the flour, salt, and pepper on a dinner plate. Break the egg into a shallow bowl and beat until frothy. Put the panko and Cajun seasoning on another dinner plate and stir to combine.

4. Heat 1 inch of safflower oil in a small skillet or saucepan over medium-high heat until an instant-read or deep-fry thermometer registers 350°F. Crumple some paper towels and place them on a plate and set it next to the stove.

5. While the oil is heating up, bread the oysters. Gently place the oysters on the plate with the flour and spoon it over the tops of the oysters so they are evenly coated. Don't move them around too much or they'll break up into pieces. Next, gently dip the oysters in the egg, letting the excess drip off, and then place them on the plate with the panko. Spoon the panko over the tops of the oysters and press gently to adhere.

6. Fry the oysters in small batches (3 or 4 at a time), turning the oysters once, until they are golden brown and crisp, about 30 seconds per side. (Adjust the temperature as necessary; if the panko is getting dark too fast, lower the heat; if the oysters take longer than 30 to 40 seconds per side to arrive at a deep golden brown, the oil is too cold.) Transfer the fried oysters to the paper towel–lined plate as you work.

7. Divide the oysters among the tortillas (about 3 per tortilla). Mound the remoulade on top and sprinkle with the jalapeno chips. Serve immediately.

TACO TIPS

If you're not an oyster fan, substitute a pound of raw, peeled, and deveined shrimp and follow the recipe as instructed, adding about 4 minutes to the cook time.

Pork Tenderloin Tacos with Tomatillo-Avocado Salsa

SERVES 4 (MAKES 8 TACOS)

Braised pork shoulder with tomatillo-based sauce is a mainstay of taco establishments far and wide, but sometimes I'm in the mood for something a little leaner that cooks a lot quicker. Enter grilled pork tenderloin! Marinate the tender meat in an easy mix of smoky chipotle peppers, orange juice, and a touch of oregano and cinnamon for a seriously delicious taco. The bright, slightly acidic Tomatillo Salsa (page 108) plus avocado is the perfect foil for the sweetness of the pork. I like to sprinkle crushed pork rinds (plain or chile-seasoned) over the top of the tacos for a lovely crunch, but it's optional.

INGREDIENTS

1 (1- to 1½-pound) pork tenderloin, trimmed (see Taco Tips)

¼ cup finely chopped canned chipotle chile pepper in adobo

¼ cup fresh orange juice

¼ cup safflower oil

2 tablespoons oregano (preferably Mexican oregano)

2 teaspoons ground cinnamon

2 teaspoons granulated garlic powder

1 tablespoon salt

2 teaspoons black pepper

1 cup Tomatillo Salsa (page 108), or jarred green salsa

1 ripe avocado, diced

8 (6-inch) homemade corn tortillas (page 3), half and half tortillas (page 7), or flour tortillas (page 9), or store-bought tortillas, warmed

½ cup pickled red onions (page 118)

1 cup coarsely crushed pork rinds

INSTRUCTIONS

1. Stab the tenderloin all over with a paring knife. Combine the chipotle chile, orange juice, oil, oregano, cinnamon, garlic powder, salt, and pepper in a small bowl. Rub the mixture all over the tenderloin. Place in a non-reactive container, cover, and let tenderloin marinate for at least 1 hour or up to 24 hours in the refrigerator.

2. Preheat a grill over medium-high heat. Place the tenderloin on the grill, and cook uncovered, turning occasionally, until an instant-read thermometer registers 145°F for juicy, slightly rosy (but completely safe) meat, 12 to 18 minutes. Transfer the pork to a cutting board and cover loosely with foil and let it rest for 10 minutes.

3. In a medium bowl, combine the tomatillo salsa and the avocado and set aside. Slice the tenderloin crosswise and then roughly chop the meat into bite-size pieces. Divide the pork among the tortillas. Top with the tomatillo-avocado salsa, pickled onions, and a sprinkle of the crushed pork rinds. Serve immediately.

TACO TIPS

If you buy untrimmed pork tenderloin, it will have a thin layer of silvery connective tissue just under the surface. Be sure to remove this with a thin-bladed knife before cooking; it's quite tough. Pork tenderloins often come in packs of two; I usually coat the second tenderloin with a little of the marinade and freeze it for future tacos.

Quinoa and Veggie Double Tacos with Guacamole

SERVES 4 (MAKES 8 TACOS)

Double tacos are a novel taco idea I picked up while working at Pasqual's Cantina, a great little taco shop in Madison, Wisconsin. Just spread a warm flour tortilla with guacamole, put a crunchy taco in the middle of that, fill it with goodness, and then sandwich the two together. You'll get a kaleidoscope of textures and flavors—chewy flour tortilla, creamy-spicy guacamole, and then crunchiness from the hard-shell taco inside.

I fill the tacos with a protein-rich vegetarian quinoa and veggie filling that's baked in an easy-peasy casserole here. The casserole can be assembled up to 2 days ahead and baked when you are ready to eat, so it's a great weeknight meal prep dinner for busy nights.

INGREDIENTS

1 red bell pepper, seeded and chopped

1 medium zucchini, chopped

½ cup quinoa, rinsed and drained

½ teaspoon salt

1½ cups homemade A Batch of Really Good Black Beans (page 123) or 1 (15-ounce) can black beans, drained and rinsed

2 teaspoons Tajin seasoning

1¼ teaspoons cumin

½ teaspoon oregano (preferably Mexican oregano)

½ cup Roasted Tomato Jalapeno Salsa (page 110), or pico de gallo (page 106), plus more for serving

1 cup shredded Cheddar cheese

8 crispy corn taco shells

2 medium avocados, halved and pitted

1 tablespoon hot sauce (such as Truff Black Truffle Hot Sauce)

8 (6-inch) homemade flour tortillas (page 9), or store-bought, warmed

INSTRUCTIONS

1. Preheat the oven to 350°F. Spray an 8 x 8-inch square baking dish with cooking spray. Add the bell pepper and zucchini in an even layer and set aside.

2. Put the quinoa and salt in a small saucepan. Add 1 cup of water and bring to a boil over high heat. Cover, reduce heat to low, and simmer for 10 minutes. Turn off heat and let quinoa stand, covered, for 5 minutes. Pour quinoa into a medium bowl and add the beans, Tajin seasoning, cumin, and oregano.

3. Spread the quinoa mixture over the vegetables in the baking dish. Spoon the salsa over the quinoa. Top with the cheese and bake until the cheese has melted, and the mixture is hot throughout, 30 minutes. Remove from the oven.

4. Put the hard taco shells on a small baking sheet and bake until golden brown on the edges and warmed, 5 minutes. Meanwhile, mash the avocado flesh with the hot sauce and spread on the flour tortillas.

5. Fill the warm, crispy tortilla shells with the quinoa mixture. Put the crispy tacos in the center of the avocado-spread flour tortillas and bring up the sides so the avocado sticks to the crispy shells. Top with additional salsa, if desired.

TACO TIPS

Not into quinoa? Substitute cooked freekeh, bulgur, or brown rice for the cooked quinoa (you'll need 1¼ cups).

Royale with Cheese Tacos

SERVES 4 (MAKES 8 TACOS)

A spin on a certain fast-food chain's double-layer burger with its very own jingle, this taco boasts beef patties, special sauce, lettuce, pickles, onions, and cheese in the form of a delicious crisp. (Sprinkle it with sesame seeds if you're really sticking to the script.)

To achieve the crusty, slightly charred exterior of these burgers, you've got to embrace the heat and cook them in a smoking-hot pan. Just remember to turn on the exhaust fan, open a window, and don't be afraid of a little smoke.

INGREDIENTS

For the "special" sauce:
¼ cup good-quality mayonnaise (such as Duke's or Kewpie)

2 tablespoons ketchup

1 tablespoon finely chopped dill pickle chips

1¼ teaspoons sugar

1 teaspoon white wine vinegar or pickle brine

For the tacos:
½ cup finely chopped white onion

1¾ pounds ground beef chuck (85% lean)

2 cups finely grated mild Cheddar or Colby Jack cheese

1 teaspoon seasoning salt (such as Johnny's Seasoning Salt)

8 (6-inch) homemade flour tortillas (page 9) or half and half tortillas (page 7), warmed

2 cups finely shredded iceberg or romaine lettuce

16 dill pickle chips, cut into bite-size pieces

2 tablespoons toasted sesame seeds (optional)

INSTRUCTIONS

1. Mix the mayonnaise, ketchup, dill pickle, sugar, and vinegar together. Cover and refrigerate until needed. Put the chopped onions in a bowl with cold water for 10 minutes, drain, and set aside (soaking the onions will remove some of their bitterness).

2. Divide the beef into 4 equal portions (about 7 to 8 ounces each), and then pat them into roughly 6-inch patties. Put the patties in the refrigerator for at least 10 minutes.

3. Line a small baking sheet with paper towels. Heat a large, nonstick skillet over medium-high heat. When the pan is very hot, sprinkle ½ cup of the grated cheese into the pan to create a round that is roughly 5-inches in diameter; there will be small spaces between the bits of cheese—don't worry, they will disappear as the cheese melts. Use a silicone spatula to neaten up the edges and coax any stray cheese bits into the circle. Cook on 1 side until browned, 1 minute. Flip and cook on the second side until crispy, 30 seconds. Transfer to the paper towels and repeat with remaining cheese to make 4 cheese crisps. Cut the rounds in half with a sharp knife and set aside.

4. Heat a large cast-iron pan or heavy skillet over high heat until almost smoking (or use the pan you made the cheese crisps in). Put the beef patties in the pan and sprinkle with half of the seasoning salt. Press down on the burgers with a spatula as soon as they hit the pan to squish them down a little, and then cook for 2 minutes without touching them. (Do not crowd the burgers or they won't brown properly; you may need to cook them in batches or use 2 pans.)

5. Flip the burgers, sprinkle with the remaining seasoning salt, and cook on the second side until the meat is no longer red in the center when you nick and peek, 1½ to 2 minutes. Transfer the burgers to a cutting board and cut each patty in half.

6. Hold a tortilla in your hand in a taco shape and put a half cheese crisp and a half burger patty (cut sides toward the bottom of the tortilla). Top with special sauce, onions, lettuce, and pickles. Sprinkle on sesame seeds, if desired. Repeat with remaining tortillas and fillings. Serve right away.

TACO TIPS

Make the meal vegetarian by using 4 veggie burgers and cooking them in a hot, well-oiled pan.

(And yes, the "Royale with Cheese" is a *Pulp Fiction* movie reference.)

Seafood Ceviche Tacos

SERVES 4 (MAKES 8 TACOS)

Too hot to cook? This fresh, citrusy seafood taco is the answer to your dinnertime woes. Marinating raw seafood in citrus juice "cooks" the proteins in the fish and shellfish. It may look like a lot of lime juice in the recipe, but it's key to submerge the fish in citrus and marinate it for an hour to get the right texture. Be sure to use the best quality marine (ocean-dwelling) fish for this recipe and buy it from a reputable seafood market (see Taco Tips). The red peppercorns add a fruity, peppery pop to the ceviche, so don't skip them!

INGREDIENTS

10 ounces fresh marine fish such as ahi tuna, halibut, or mahi mahi

10 ounces wild peeled and deveined shrimp or bay scallops

⅔ cup freshly squeezed lime juice (from about 4 limes)

1 large shallot, thinly sliced

1 small serrano chile pepper, very thinly sliced

1 small garlic clove, minced

½ teaspoon salt, plus more for seasoning

¼ cup mild olive oil

3 tablespoons chopped cilantro

1 tablespoon Tajin seasoning

1 teaspoon coarsely ground red peppercorns

8 (6-inch) crispy taco shells

1 large avocado, halved lengthwise, pitted, and cut into thin slices

INSTRUCTIONS

1. Pat the seafood dry. Trim away any silvery connective tissue that might be on the fish. Cut the fish and shrimp into small (½-inch) chunks and put them in a medium non-reactive bowl. Add the lime juice, shallot, serrano pepper, garlic, and salt and toss to combine. Cover and refrigerate for 1 hour.

2. Drain the seafood in a fine mesh sieve, discarding the liquid. Put the seafood back in the non-reactive bowl and add the olive oil, cilantro, Tajín, and red peppercorns. Season with additional salt to taste. Let the ceviche stand for at least 10 minutes or up to 8 hours refrigerated to let the flavors mingle.

3. Preheat the oven to 350°F. Put the taco shells on a small, rimmed baking sheet and bake until the edges are golden brown and they are warm, 5 minutes. Put sliced avocado in the bottom of each tortilla shell and then mound the ceviche into the tortillas. Serve immediately.

TACO TIPS

Ask your fishmonger for "sushi grade" fish for use in a raw preparation. While it's technically only a marketing term, it usually indicates that the fish is very fresh and suitable to be eaten raw.

That '70s Taco

A nostalgic throwback—these tacos are stuffed with ground turkey sautéed with homemade taco seasoning, iceberg lettuce, crispy Tater Tots, and drizzles of nacho cheese sauce spiked with pickled jalapeno juice. Easy, economical, and divinely comforting, here's an American taco that will take you back to the days of bell-bottoms and *The Brady Bunch* (Google it).

Making your own taco seasoning is very rewarding and it keeps for months, though it won't last that long—you'll be using it on everything. (Hint: popcorn!) This recipe makes enough taco seasoning for 2 batches of this recipe.

INGREDIENTS

For the homemade taco seasoning:
2 tablespoons mild chili powder (such as Gebhardt's)

2 teaspoons ground cumin

2 teaspoons brown sugar

1½ teaspoons granulated garlic powder

1½ teaspoons onion powder

1 teaspoon salt

½ teaspoon pepper

½ teaspoon oregano (preferably Mexican oregano)

½ teaspoon MSG (optional)

¼ teaspoon cayenne pepper

For the tacos:
2 cups frozen tater tots

8 crunchy corn tortilla taco shells

1 tablespoon safflower oil

81

1 pound ground turkey (preferably a mix of dark and breast meat), or lean ground beef

2 tablespoons tomato paste

½ cup water

3 cups finely shredded iceberg lettuce

½ cup chopped tomatoes

¼ cup pickled jalapeno slices

For the cheese sauce:

½ cup heavy whipping cream

4 slices American cheese (4 ounces)

½ cup grated Colby Jack cheese

1 tablespoon pickled jalapeno juice, or lemon juice

Salt to taste

INSTRUCTIONS

1. Preheat the oven to 425°F. In a small bowl, combine the taco seasoning ingredients, and pour into a clean spice jar or airtight container. Put the tater tots on a rimmed baking sheet and sprinkle with 1 teaspoon of the seasoning. Bake until golden brown, stirring once, 15 to 20 minutes. The last 5 minutes of cooking, add the taco shells to the edges of the baking sheet to lightly toast them.

2. Meanwhile, make the meat filling. Heat the oil in a large skillet over medium-high heat. Add the turkey and 4 teaspoons of the taco seasoning and cook, breaking the meat up with a spatula, until the turkey is browned, 5 minutes. Add the tomato paste and cook, stirring constantly, until it begins to brown, 1 minute. Add the water and simmer until the liquid evaporates by half, 3 minutes. Reduce heat to low and keep warm.

3. In a small saucepan, bring the cream to a simmer over medium heat. Reduce heat to low and add the cheeses gradually, one big pinch at a time, whisking after each addition. Add the jalapeno juice or lemon juice and whisk to combine. Remove from heat and let stand for 5 minutes; the mixture will thicken as it cools.

4. Divide the meat mixture among the taco shells. Top with the lettuce, tomatoes, jalapeno slices, and about 4 tater tots per taco (reserve remaining tots for serving with any leftover cheese sauce). Spoon the cheese sauce over the tacos and serve right away.

TACO TIPS

Toasting store-bought crispy corn tortilla shells for a few minutes will transform them from ho-hum school cafeteria fare to crispy, corny revelations.

Umami Tacos

SERVES **4** (MAKES **8** ABOUT TACOS)

Every time you bite into a juicy steak, sample a dish with wild mushrooms, or nibble corn on the cob, you're experiencing umami, the "meaty" or "savory" flavor sensation that is found in foods that are high in naturally occurring amino acids called glutamates. In this ultra-umami taco, maple-roasted shiitake mushrooms add an incredible "meaty" flavor and chew. A simple sauté of corn, onion, and poblano rounds out the umami, while homemade beans add protein.

Instead of sour cream or other dairy-based sauce, these vegan tacos get a drizzle of cashew-based Roasted Garlic Crema (page 115), which will change your taco game forever. With these delicious flavors combined into a taco, no one will ever guess they're eating a 100 percent plant-based meal!

INGREDIENTS

For the shiitake "bacon":

8 ounces thinly sliced shiitake mushrooms, stems discarded (about 2 cups)

4 teaspoons dark sesame oil

1 tablespoon safflower or olive oil

1 tablespoon maple syrup

½ teaspoon garlic powder

½ teaspoon smoked paprika

½ teaspoon salt

¼ teaspoon pepper

For the corn sauté and tacos:

2 tablespoons olive oil

1 large poblano chile pepper, seeded and finely chopped (see Taco Tips)

½ medium yellow onion, chopped

2 ears sweet corn, shucked, kernels shaved from the cob

2 teaspoons Homemade Taco Seasoning (page 81, That '70s Taco), or store-bought taco blend

3 tablespoons lime juice

Salt to taste

1½ cups A Batch of Really Good Black Beans (page 123) or 1 (15-ounce) can black beans, drained and rinsed

8 to 12 (6-inch) homemade flour tortillas (page 9), corn tortillas (page 3), or store-bought tortillas, warmed

½ cup Roasted Garlic Crema (page 115)

INSTRUCTIONS

1. Preheat the oven to 375°F. Line a baking sheet with parchment paper. Spray with cooking spray. Toss the mushrooms with the oils, syrup, garlic powder, paprika, salt, and pepper. The raw mushrooms will look like a lot, but they'll intensify in flavor and shrink as they roast. Arrange the mushrooms in a single layer on the baking sheet and bake, stirring occasionally, until they have shrunk, and the edges begin to crisp, about 20 to 25 minutes.

2. To make the corn filling, heat the oil in a large skillet over medium heat. Add the poblano chile and onion and sauté, stirring frequently, until the vegetables begin to brown, 5 minutes. Add the corn and taco seasoning and cook, stirring constantly, for 1 minute. Add 3 tablespoons of water and stir. Cover and simmer until the poblano pepper is tender, 5 minutes. Add the lime juice and cook uncovered, scraping up the browned bits on the bottom of the pan, until the liquid has evaporated, 2 minutes. Remove from heat and season with salt to taste.

3. Divide the corn mixture, beans, and shiitake "bacon" evenly among the tortillas. Drizzle with the crema and serve.

TACO TIPS

Taste the poblano chile pepper as you slice it. Peppers get hotter toward the stem and seed end, and some poblanos can be quite hot.

Vindaloo Pork Tacos

SERVES **8** (MAKES ABOUT **16** TACOS)

A dish born of the Portuguese invasion and occupation of the southwestern Indian state of Goa, the name vindaloo is a mash-up of *vin* and *d'ahlo*, wine and garlic, and that's what this dish delivers. Goanese cooks have made the dish their own since then, braising meat with vinegar, garlic, and plenty of chilies and spices thrown in for good measure.

This recipe is adapted from my dear friend Leena Ezekiel, an incredible chef and founder of Thali Supper Club, a pop-up with a huge following in Portland, Oregon. Yes, this recipe takes a bit of time, but the recipe is broken into 2 parts: the first for grinding spices and marinating the pork, the second for braising the meat. The result is melt-in-your-mouth pork in a soulful, not-too-hot sauce that's an ideal filling for tacos. Topped with Cilantro Lime Crema (page 113), it's as close to Goa as you can get without a 23-hour plane ride.

INGREDIENTS

For the vindaloo spice paste and pork:

15 green cardamom pods

4 to 6 dried red chiles de arbol, stems discarded

2 teaspoons whole cumin seeds

1½ teaspoons brown mustard seeds

1 teaspoon black peppercorns

1 (3-inch) stick of cinnamon

1 teaspoon fenugreek seeds

1½ teaspoons salt

1 teaspoon brown sugar

5 tablespoons white wine vinegar

1 cup vegetable oil

1 large white onion, thinly sliced

2½ pounds pork shoulder, trimmed and cut into 1-inch cubes

For the pork and tacos:

2 tablespoons finely chopped fresh ginger

12 garlic cloves, peeled (see Taco Tips)

2 tablespoons of the oil used to fry the onions from marinade

1 large white onion, finely chopped

1 tablespoon ground coriander

1 teaspoon turmeric

Salt to taste

Cayenne to taste

8 (6-inch) homemade flour tortillas (page 9), or corn tortillas (page 3), or
store-bought tortillas, warmed

½ cup chopped cilantro

½ cup Cilantro Lime Crema (page 113), or plain Greek yogurt

INSTRUCTIONS

1. The day before you plan to eat, marinate the pork. Place the cardamom pods on a cutting board and crack them open with the bottom of a juice glass. Put the black seeds in an electric spice/coffee grinder or mortar and pestle; discard outer cardamom pods. Add the chiles, cumin seeds, brown mustard seeds, black peppercorns, cinnamon stick, fenugreek seeds, salt, and brown sugar and grind until fine powder. Put the ground spices in a medium non-reactive bowl. Add the vinegar and set aside.

2. Heat the oil in a large sauté pan over medium heat. Add the onions and cook, stirring frequently and scraping down the sides of the pan, until the onions are browned and crispy, about 18 to 20 minutes. (Watch carefully so the onions don't burn.) Remove from heat. Transfer the onions with a slotted spoon to paper towel–lined plate. Reserve the oil.

3. Put the onions in a blender or food processor, add 2 or 3 tablespoons water, and process until smooth. Add the onion puree to the ground spice mixture and stir to combine. Add the pork and stir to coat. Cover and marinate overnight in the refrigerator.

4. The next day, braise the pork. Combine the ginger and garlic cloves with a few tablespoons of water in a mini food processor and whizz them until you have a fine paste; set aside.

5. Heat 2 tablespoons of the reserved onion oil in a large Dutch oven or saucepan over medium heat. (Reserve the remaining onion oil for another use.) Add the chopped onions and cook, stirring frequently, until the onions are golden brown, 10 minutes. Add the ginger-garlic paste and cook, stirring constantly, until fragrant, 20 seconds. Add about half of the pork and cook until browned in places, 5 minutes. Add the coriander and turmeric and stir to combine. Add the remaining pork and 1 cup of water to the pan and bring to a simmer over medium-high heat.

6. Cover, reduce heat to low, and simmer, stirring occasionally and scraping the sides of the pan to make sure all the caramelized goodness is returned to the sauce, until the pork is fork-tender, 1½ hours. Uncover the pan and continue to simmer for 30 minutes to reduce and thicken the sauce. Season with salt to taste and add cayenne powder, if desired.

7. Using a slotted spoon, divide the pork among the tortillas. Top with the cilantro, drizzle with the crema, and serve immediately.

TACO TIPS

If you don't relish the idea of peeling a whole head of garlic, substitute pre-peeled garlic cloves, available in bags in the produce department of some grocery stores.

You can also use ready-made dry vindaloo masala spice powder instead of grinding your own spices; I like Penzeys Vindaloo masala.

Watercress and Flank Steak Thai-Inspired Tacos

SERVES 4 (MAKES 8 TACOS)

This recipe is inspired by an awesome steak and fresh herb salad I learned to make with Chef Sompon Nabnian at the Chiang Mai Thai Cookery School. The hot, salty, sour, sweet "salsa" features peppery watercress, Thai bird chilies, fish sauce, lime juice, and palm sugar, which play off the savory flavor of tender grilled flank steak and fistfuls of fresh herbs.

Be sure to buy plenty of fresh herbs to stuff the tacos—they're not just a garnish, but a key part of the meal, and part of what makes this taco so fresh-tasting. You'll get the best deal on bags of herbs at Asian markets. I like to serve this meal family-style, letting folks build their own tacos with the ingredients served on a platter.

INGREDIENTS

For the salsa:

½ bunch watercress, large stems discarded

1 cup cilantro with the stems (loosely packed)

1 large clove garlic, sliced

Zest and juice of 1 lime

1 to 2 red Thai bird chilies, finely chopped with or without seeds (adjust according to your spice tolerance)

1 tablespoon fish sauce

2 teaspoons palm sugar or brown sugar

2 tablespoons safflower oil

1 small, ripe tomato, seeded and chopped

¼ cup chopped roasted, salted peanuts

For the tacos:

1 pound beef flank steak

½ teaspoon salt

2 tablespoons canned Thai red curry paste (such as Mae Ploy)

2 tablespoons safflower oil

2 cups fresh, tender green herbs (watercress and cilantro, plus mint, chives, basil)

½ cucumber, thinly sliced

⅓ cup thinly sliced shallots

8 (6-inch) homemade corn tortillas (page 3), warmed

INSTRUCTIONS

1. Combine the watercress, cilantro, garlic, lime zest and juice, bird chile, fish sauce, palm or brown sugar, and oil in a blender and blend until smooth. Pour into a bowl. Stir in the tomato and peanuts. Taste and adjust seasoning, adding fish sauce or lime juice, if needed, to balance the flavors. Set aside for at least 10 minutes to allow flavors to meld.

2. Season the steak all over with the salt. Combine the curry paste and oil in a small bowl and rub the mixture all over the meat. Set aside to marinate while you preheat a gas or charcoal grill, or a grill pan over medium-high heat.

3. Place the steak on the grill or pan and cook for 3½ minutes per side, or until medium-rare. (An instant-read thermometer inserted into the steak horizontally will read 135°F.) Transfer the steak to a cutting board and let the meat rest for 10 minutes.

4. Thinly slice the steak across the grain and arrange it on a serving platter. Spoon the salsa over the steak and scatter with the herbs, cucumber, and shallots. Serve family-style, with warm tortillas for build-your-own tacos.

TACO TIPS

Bird chilies (sometimes labeled *prik kee noo* in Thai markets) are small (1- to 1½-inch-long) chilies that come in bags of way more chilies than you'll need for this recipe. Fortunately, they freeze well and can be used while still frozen. Their fruity-hot flavor makes them indispensable for Thai food lovers. Be sure to use gloves when handling them—they can pack a punch.

XO Shrimp and Cheese Toasty Tacos

SERVES 4 (MAKES 8 TACOS)

The combo of shrimp, peppers, onions, and melted cheese in these tacos is inspired by *tacos al gobernadora*, a specialty of the western Mexican state of Sinaloa. To ramp up the sweet shrimp flavor, I add a thick condiment called XO sauce.

XO is an umami-packed ingredient invented in Hong Kong in the '80s and includes ingredients like dried shrimp, scallops, and ham blended into a thick paste with aromatic shallots and chilies. XO adds heaps of flavor to everything it touches (asparagus stir-fry #FTW). It's named after premium XO Cognac, theoretically adding prestige to the condiment by association, though it contains no brandy. Look for XO at Asian markets and some supermarkets. I like Lee Kum Kee's brand, but a lot of indie food companies are breaking into the market with their own versions of the trendy condiment, so I encourage you to experiment!

INGREDIENTS

1½ tablespoons olive oil

1 large shallot, thinly sliced (about ½ cup)

1 red bell pepper, seeded and finely chopped

2 Roma tomatoes, seeded and chopped

3 tablespoons XO sauce (see Taco Tips)

½ teaspoon dried oregano (preferably Mexican oregano)

1 pound peeled and deveined shrimp, roughly chopped

1 to 2 tablespoons chopped canned chipotle chilies in adobo

2 tablespoons sour cream

2 tablespoons chopped cilantro

Salt and pepper to taste

8 ounces (2½ cups) shredded Monterey Jack cheese

8 (6-inch) homemade flour tortillas (page 9), or half and half tortillas (pages 7), or store-bought flour tortillas

INSTRUCTIONS

1.   Heat the olive oil in a large nonstick sauté pan over medium-high heat. Add the shallot and bell pepper and sauté, stirring frequently, until the vegetables are tender, 3 minutes. Add the tomatoes, XO sauce, and oregano and cook, stirring frequently, until the tomatoes soften, 3 minutes.

2.   Add the shrimp and chipotle chilies and cook, stirring occasionally, until the shrimp are just cooked, 3 minutes. Scrape the shrimp mixture into a bowl. Stir in the sour cream and cilantro. Season with salt and pepper to taste.

3.   Rinse out the pan and return the pan to medium-high heat. Heat a second large pan or skillet over medium-high heat. Arrange 2 to 3 tortillas in each of the dry pans. (You will need to work in batches.) Sprinkle each tortilla evenly with about ⅓ cup of cheese (a little cheese escaping around the edges of each tortilla will provide you with lovely crispy bits) and cook until the cheese has melted, 1 minute.

4.   Spoon the shrimp mixture on one half of each tortilla. Fold the shrimpless side of the tortilla over the filling to fold the tortilla in half. Push down gently with a spatula to sandwich the sides together. Repeat with remaining tortillas, cheese, and shrimp filling. Serve immediately.

TACO TIPS

No XO? No problem. You can make a very rough substitute by mixing 2 tablespoons of oyster sauce with 1 tablespoon chili crisp condiment. But I do recommend you find XO sauce someday. It's awesome stuff.

Yellowtail Tacos with Mango-Avocado Salsa

SERVES 4 (MAKES 8 TACOS)

Yellowtail is a meaty Pacific fish from the jack family. It's prized by sushi lovers for its rich-but-not-fishy flavor and delicate texture. It's delicious coated with coarsely crushed coriander seeds and seared rare to medium-rare. Look for fresh or frozen yellowtail fillets at Asian supermarkets or ask your fishmonger (see Taco Tips). A creamy spicy-sweet mango and avocado salsa plus a sprinkle of crunchy, buttery macadamia nuts complete this tropical vacation-themed taco.

INGREDIENTS

For the salsa:

1 ripe mango
1 ripe avocado, diced
2 tablespoons finely chopped shallot
1 habanero chile, seeded and chopped
1 tablespoon lime juice
Salt to taste

For the tacos:

1 pound yellowtail or ahi tuna loin, about ¾ inches thick
2 teaspoons coriander seeds
½ teaspoon salt
¼ teaspoon pepper
1 tablespoon safflower oil
8 (6-inch) homemade corn tortillas (page 3), half and half tortillas (page 7), or store-bought tortillas, warmed
½ cup chopped, salted roasted macadamia nuts

INSTRUCTIONS

1. With the slender side of the mango facing you, cut the fleshy sides of the mango away from the pit in the center (the pit is about ½-inch thick; you'll hear a fibrous crunch if your knife is too close to it). With the cut side of mango facing you, use a paring knife to cut a crisscross pattern into the flesh without cutting through the peel. Gently push the mango from the back side to invert the fruit so the mango flesh is pushed forward. Use the knife to cut the flesh cubes away from the peel. Repeat with the other half of the mango. Place in a small bowl. Add the avocado, shallot, habanero, and lime juice and stir to combine. Season with salt and set aside.

2. Pat the fish dry. Heat a large cast-iron skillet or sauté pan over medium heat. Add the coriander seeds and toast them in the dry pan, swirling occasionally, until they are aromatic, 3 minutes. Crush the seeds in a mortar and pestle or with the bottom of a small pan until they are coarsely crushed. Mix the coriander seeds, salt, and pepper in a small bowl. Spread the spice mixture all over the fish, pressing gently to adhere.

3. Heat the large cast-iron skillet used to toast the seeds over high heat. Add the oil and, when it's very hot, add the fish. Cook until the fish is seared on both sides but still pink in the center, about 2 minutes per side. Transfer the fish to a cutting board and carve it into thin slices. To help keep each piece from falling apart, cut the fish fillets against the grain into thin slices with a sharp carving knife held at a slight angle.

4. Divide the fish among the tortillas and top with the mango-avocado salsa. Sprinkle with the macadamia nuts and serve immediately.

TACO TIPS

If you can't find yellowtail, try the recipe using another firm marine fish such as ahi tuna or swordfish.

Z a'atar Chicken Tacos

SERVES 4 (MAKES 8 TACOS)

Inspired by my very talented friend Mirna Attar, chef of Ya Hala restaurant in Portland, Oregon, this recipe stars za'atar marinated grilled chicken folded into flour tortillas crowned with vibrant pickled cabbage and creamy roasted garlic crema. It's a shawarma-meets-taco mash-up that ticks all the boxes—easy, quick, and off-the-charts tasty.

INGREDIENTS

⅓ cup lemon juice

3 tablespoons olive oil

4 teaspoons za'atar, plus more for garnish (see Taco Tips)

2 medium garlic cloves, chopped

½ teaspoon salt

½ teaspoon ground black pepper

1½ pounds boneless, skinless chicken breasts, sliced crosswise into ½-inch strips

8 (6-inch) homemade flour tortillas (page 9), or store-bought tortillas, warmed

3 cups Pickled Red Cabbage (page 119)

½ cup Roasted Garlic Crema (page 115)

INSTRUCTIONS

1. Line a baking sheet with foil. In a large non-reactive bowl, combine the lemon juice, olive oil, za'atar, garlic, salt, and pepper. Set aside 2 tablespoons of the marinade. Add the chicken to the remaining marinade and stir to combine. Set aside to marinate the chicken for at least 30 minutes and up to overnight in the refrigerator.

2. Preheat the broiler on high and adjust the oven rack so it is 4 inches below the broiler element. Arrange the chicken strips on the foil-lined baking sheet; discard marinade that the chicken was in. Broil, turning once with tongs, until the meat is cooked through and charred in places, about 3 minutes per side. Remove the chicken from the pan and toss with the reserved marinade.

3. Divide the chicken among the tortillas and sprinkle with additional za'atar. Top with the pickled red cabbage mixture and drizzle with the roasted garlic crema. Serve immediately.

TACO TIPS

Za'atar is both a wild herb that grows in the Middle East and a blend of herbs including sumac, oregano, sesame seeds, and even edible flower petals occasionally! It has an alluring, musky flavor that pairs especially well with grilled meats. Look for it at well-stocked markets or online. I like cookbook author Maureen Abood's za'atar blend, available at www.maureenaboodmarket.com.

CHAPTER 3

SALSAS, SAUCES, PICKLES, AND BEANS

Pico de Gallo

This chunky tomato salsa, literally "beak of the rooster," is all about freshness; it is best when made from scratch and eaten the day it's made. Look for ripe, plump tomatoes that have never seen the inside of the refrigerator (cold temperatures make tomato flesh mealy). Be sure to scoop out the seeds from the tomatoes as you chop them, or the salsa will be watery, which equals soggy tacos. You can make the salsa milder by removing the seeds and pale inner ribs from the jalapeno.

INGREDIENTS

2 large, ripe tomatoes (about 1 pound)

¼ medium red onion, thinly sliced

1 small jalapeno chile, thinly sliced, core and stem discarded

¼ cup cilantro leaves

1 medium garlic clove, sliced

1 teaspoon salt

1 tablespoon lime juice

1 tablespoon olive oil

Freshly ground black pepper (optional)

INSTRUCTIONS

1.   Cut the tomatoes into wedges, poke out the seeds with your fingers, and discard. Finely chop the tomatoes and put them in a large non-reactive bowl.

2.   Mound the onion, jalapeno, cilantro, garlic, and salt on a cutting board. Chop together until everything is in tiny pieces and the mixture looks wet and broken down. The easiest way to do this is to balance your non-dominant hand on the top of the knife to steady it as you use your dominant hand to move the knife around. Transfer to the bowl with the tomatoes.

3.   Add the lime juice and olive oil and stir to combine. Add additional salt and pepper, if desired. Serve within 4 hours.

TACO TIPS

The fresh salsa is very adaptable. Substitute fresh nectarines or peaches for the tomatoes, use serrano or red jalapeno for a different kind of spicy heat, or add a splash of fish sauce instead of salt for an umami hit. In short, make it yours.

Tomatillo Salsa

MAKES ABOUT **2** CUPS

If you've never made your own green salsa before, you are in for a treat! Just broil tomatillos with onion, a chile pepper, and some garlic and throw it in a blender. You'll be rewarded with a fresh, tangy salsa that's good on everything from pork (see page 67, Pork Tenderloin Tacos with Tomatillo-Avocado Salsa) to grilled fish, or a good ol' bowl of tortilla chips.

INGREDIENTS

1¼ pounds fresh tomatillos (about 12 large), or 1 (28-ounce) can tomatillos, drained
½ white onion, cut into thick slices
1 Anaheim chile pepper
6 large garlic cloves, papery outer skin discarded, inner skin left on
1 tablespoon olive oil
¼ cup chopped cilantro
1 tablespoon lime juice
Zest of 1 lime
1 teaspoon ground coriander seeds
1 teaspoon sugar
Salt, to taste

INSTRUCTIONS

1. Heat broiler on high with the oven rack in topmost position. Line a rimmed baking sheet with foil.

2. Remove the husks and stems from the tomatillos. Put the tomatillos, onion, Anaheim chile, and garlic on the baking sheet and toss with the oil. Broil until everything is charred, turning ingredients once with tongs, 8 to 10 minutes. Set aside to cool for a few minutes.

3. Remove the skins from the garlic and discard. Remove the skin, seeds, and stem from the chile and discard. Put the vegetables, along with juices on the pan, in a blender or food processor. Add the cilantro, lime juice, lime zest, coriander, and sugar and blend until mostly smooth. Season with salt to taste. Pour the salsa into a bowl and serve, or once cool, store in an airtight container for up to 1 week.

TACO TIPS

If the tomatillo husks prove difficult to remove, soak the tomatillos in a bowl of hot tap water for 10 minutes and then rub the husks away with your fingers.

Roasted Tomato Jalapeno Salsa

MAKES 2½ CUPS

This quick tomato blender salsa has a lovely high note of heat from jalapeno and garlic and a touch of sweet smokiness because the vegetables are broiled before blending. This thick, smooth salsa will last at least a week in the refrigerator, but be warned, it will get hotter with time.

INGREDIENTS

1 pound ripe Roma tomatoes, cut in half lengthwise

1 jalapeno chile pepper, stem discarded, halved lengthwise

¼ medium yellow onion, thickly sliced

6 large garlic cloves, papery outer skins discarded, inner skin left on

½ cup cilantro leaves (loosely packed)

1 tablespoon lime juice

1 teaspoon ground cumin

½ teaspoon sugar

½ teaspoon salt, plus more for seasoning

INSTRUCTIONS

1. Adjust oven rack so it is 6 inches (second-highest position) below broiling element and preheat broiler on high. Line a rimmed baking sheet with foil and spray lightly with cooking spray.

2. Place the tomatoes and jalapeno pepper cut side down on the baking sheet and nestle the slices of onion and garlic around them. Broil until the vegetables are lightly charred on top and they have begun to collapse, 15 minutes.

3. Remove the baking sheet from the oven and set aside to cool for 10 minutes. If you prefer a milder salsa, scrape out and discard some (or all) of the pepper seeds. Peel the skins from the garlic and discard.

4. Transfer the broiled vegetables to a blender or food processor. Add the cilantro, lime, cumin, sugar, and salt and blend until smooth. Taste and add salt, if desired. Pour the salsa into a serving bowl and serve immediately, or store in a non-reactive container in the refrigerator for up to 1 week.

TACO TIPS

Look for Roma tomatoes that feel heavy for their size, are deep red, and smell aromatic when sniffed near the stem end. If the Romas at the store look uninspiring, opt for vine tomatoes instead.

Cilantro Lime Crema

MAKES 1½ CUPS

This creamy green sauce is zippy enough to wake up any taco, plus it's a great way to use up less-than-fresh cilantro you might have lurking in your vegetable keeper. It keeps for up to a week in the refrigerator (base this on the "use by" date on the sour cream you use).

INGREDIENTS

1 cup sour cream
½ cup cilantro with stems (lightly packed)
¼ cup mayonnaise
2 teaspoons lime juice
1½ teaspoons Tajin seasoning
½ teaspoon salt
Zest of 1 lime, finely grated (1 teaspoon)

INSTRUCTIONS

1. Combine the ingredients in a blender or mini food processor and blend until smooth. Transfer to a squeeze bottle and store in the refrigerator for up to 1 week.

TACO TIPS

Zest the lime directly over the blender or mini food processor work bowl; the aromatic oils that are released as you grate are worth capturing.

Cilantro will wilt and become slimy if you store it in the vegetable keeper. To keep it sprightly, place it in a small glass of water, stem end down, cover loosely with a plastic bag, and keep it in the refrigerator on the top shelf.

Roasted Garlic Crema

MAKES 1¾ CUPS

This luxurious sauce is creamy and delicious just like traditional sour cream–based crema, but it's vegan! It adds a yummy savory note to tacos—and anything else you put it on. Use it as a dressing for Caesar salads, a sandwich spread, or a dip for raw veggies. It keeps for weeks in the fridge (I keep it in a squeeze bottle), but it will get used up way before that. It will separate a little when stored; just shake the bottle or whisk it vigorously to bring it back to its creamy glory.

INGREDIENTS

1 cup roasted, salted cashews
1 cup boiling water
1 large garlic head
4 tablespoons olive oil, divided
¼ cup lemon juice
1 tablespoon nutritional yeast
1 pinch cayenne pepper
Salt

INSTRUCTIONS

1. Put the cashews in a blender. Pour the boiling water over the nuts and set aside.

2. Cut the top off the head of garlic to expose the garlic cloves and drizzle with 2 tablespoons of the oil. Place the head of garlic in a small microwave-safe dish with 2 tablespoons of water. Cover with a small plate and microwave on 50 percent power for 3 minutes.

3. Remove the plate (careful, there's plenty of steam in there) and poke the center cloves with a fork. If the garlic is not very tender, re-cover, and continue to microwave the garlic on 50 percent power in 1-minute increments until the garlic is very tender.

4. Let the garlic cool and then squeeze the cloves into the blender, discarding the skins. Add the lemon juice, remaining 2 tablespoons of olive oil, nutritional yeast, and cayenne pepper and blend until smooth. Taste and add salt, if desired. Pour the sauce into a squeeze bottle or an airtight container and store in the refrigerator for up to 3 weeks.

TACO TIPS

You can also roast the garlic in the oven, though it will take longer. Preheat the oven to 350°F, drizzle the whole garlic head with the olive oil, wrap tightly in foil, and bake until tender when squeezed (about 1 hour). You can also substitute already-roasted garlic cloves, found at some grocery stores at their olive bar; you'll need about 12 cloves.

Sriracha Mayo

You can buy a bottle of premade sriracha mayonnaise, but if you're anything like me, you don't have room for yet another condiment in your fridge. This simple three-ingredient recipe makes a spicy, creamy, delicious drizzle that adds a creamy zing to any taco. The quality of the mayonnaise you use matters here, so use Duke's if you can find it. It's got a lovely, eggy flavor that is as close to the flavor of homemade mayonnaise as you can get. If that's not available, I'd recommend Kewpie brand mayonnaise, available at Asian markets and grocery stores in the know.

INGREDIENTS

½ cup mayonnaise (preferably Duke's or Kewpie)
2 tablespoons sriracha hot sauce
1 tablespoon brown sugar

INSTRUCTIONS

1. In a small bowl, whisk together the mayonnaise, hot sauce, and brown sugar. Store in an airtight container in the refrigerator for up to 1 month.

TACO TIPS

Mix this mayo with chopped ahi tuna and you're halfway to a spicy tuna roll.

Pickled Red Onions

MAKES ABOUT 2 CUPS

I was introduced to these vividly pink onions while visiting the Yucatan Peninsula, where they are often served on *cochinita pibil*, the stupendous banana leaf–wrapped marinated barbecue pork dish of the region. They're also boffo on top of tacos, salads, nachos, as a garnish for steak or bowls of beans, scrambled eggs, burgers...I can't think of any dish I don't like them on except maybe breakfast cereal. They keep indefinitely in the refrigerator and they're a snap to make.

INGREDIENTS

1 medium red onion, thinly sliced horizontally into ¼-inch-thick rings
½ cup white vinegar
4 teaspoons salt
1 tablespoon sugar
1 teaspoon coriander seeds
1 teaspoon cumin seeds
2 garlic cloves, sliced
1 bay leaf

INSTRUCTIONS

1. Put the onion slices in a clean 1-quart jar or non-reactive container.

2. Combine 2 cups of water with the vinegar, salt, sugar, coriander seeds, cumin seeds, garlic, and bay leaf in a small saucepan. Bring to a boil and simmer for 5 minutes. Pour the hot liquid over the onions and set aside at room temperature. The onions are ready within 15 minutes, but the flavor will improve with time. Once cool, cover and refrigerate for up to 3 months.

Pickled Red Cabbage

MAKES 1 QUART

Crunchy pickled red cabbage is just the thing when you'd like a little crunch on your taco but you're all out of lettuce and don't want anything as intrusive as raw onion. Be sure to slice the cabbage evenly and thinly, avoiding the tough white core of the cabbage as you slice.

INGREDIENTS

4 cups thinly sliced red cabbage

1 red jalapeno (Fresno) chile, thinly sliced

½ cup cider vinegar

4 teaspoons salt

1 tablespoon sugar

1 teaspoon coriander seeds

1 teaspoon cumin seeds

6 whole black peppercorns

2 garlic cloves, sliced

1 bay leaf

INSTRUCTIONS

1. Put the cabbage and jalapeno chile in a non-reactive container or jar, pressing down to pack it tightly into the jar.

2. In a small saucepan, bring 2 cups of water, vinegar, salt, sugar, coriander, cumin, peppercorns, garlic, and bay leaf to a boil, stirring occasionally to dissolve the sugar and salt. Pour the hot brine over the cabbage mixture, cover, and let stand at least 30 minutes before using. Once cool, cover, and refrigerate for up to 1 month. The cabbage will become hotter with time.

Refried Pinto Beans

MAKES **6** CUPS

If you've never made your own refried beans, you've never lived! The tasteless canned paste they sell as refried beans in stores is a general affront to all beans everywhere. That's a shame, because nothing makes a good taco greater than a schmear of creamy, salty, bacon-y beans. (The bacon is optional.) This recipe is a little fiddly in that you soak the beans, boil them, and then mash them in onion sautéed in bacon drippings, but the results are sublime. You'll be rewarded with a big batch of beans, enough for 3 to 4 meals, and they freeze well. Give the recipe a try and you'll never buy a can of refried beans again, promise.

INGREDIENTS

1 pound dried pinto beans, picked over for rocks or other debris

1 tablespoon salt, plus more for seasoning

2 bay leaves

1 (2-inch) piece of dried kombu or 2 tablespoons epazote (optional, see Taco Tips below)

1 tablespoon safflower oil

4 strips bacon, chopped (optional)

1 medium yellow onion, chopped

6 medium garlic cloves, chopped

Pepper, for seasoning

INSTRUCTIONS

1. Soak the beans overnight in enough water to cover the beans by 2 inches. Drain and rinse well with cool water.

2. Put the beans in a large pot and cover with enough cold water to cover the beans by 2 inches. Add the salt, bay leaves, and kombu or epazote, if using. Bring to a boil over

high heat. Cover, reduce heat to low, and simmer, stirring occasionally, until the beans are fall-apart tender, about 1½ to 2 hours.

3. Put the oil and the bacon (if using) in a large skillet or sauté pan. Cook over medium heat, stirring frequently, until the bacon is well cooked and crispy, 4 minutes. Remove the bacon with a slotted spoon and set aside.

4. Add the onions to the fat in the pan and cook, stirring frequently, until they begin to brown, 8 minutes. Add the garlic and cook until fragrant, 45 seconds. Reduce heat to low.

5. Using a slotted spoon or small sieve, scoop the pinto beans into the skillet in batches, mashing with a potato masher as you add them until all the beans have been added. Stir in enough of the cooking liquid to create a loose (even soupy) mash, about 2 cups. Cover and cook, stirring occasionally, until the flavors have melded, at least 30 minutes and ideally 1 hour.

6. Season the beans with salt and pepper and serve immediately or cool completely uncovered in the refrigerator before storing in airtight containers. The beans can be stored in the refrigerator for up to 5 days or in the freezer for up to 3 months.

TACO TIPS

If you get windy when you eat beans, you may want to try cooking the beans with a 2-inch strip of dried kombu, a type of sea kelp that is available at Asian markets and natural food stores. It's a primary ingredient in miso soup, but it can help break down the sugars in beans that make them difficult to digest.

A Batch of Really Good Black Beans

MAKES **5 CUPS**

I've said it before, and I'll say it again: beans are better from scratch. Take these black beans, simmered with aromatic onion, chipotle chile, whole cumin seeds, and bay leaf. These ingredients infuse the beans with a delicious smoky-savory flavor through and through while the long simmer ensures that you get tender, moist beans without a trace of the papery dryness that's often present in canned beans. This recipe makes plenty of beans. I usually divide the batch into 1½-cup portions (the yield of 1 can of drained beans) and store them stacked flat in freezer bags so I have beans at the ready all the time.

INGREDIENTS

1 pound dried black beans, picked over for rocks or debris
6 cups cold water
½ cup chopped white onion
1 tablespoon chopped chipotle chile in adobo
1 tablespoon salt
2 teaspoons cumin seeds
2 bay leaves

INSTRUCTIONS

1. Soak the beans overnight in enough water to cover the beans by 2 inches. Drain and rinse well with cool water.

2. Put the beans in a large pot and add the water. Add the onions, chipotle chile, salt, cumin seeds, and bay leaves. Bring to a boil over high heat. Reduce heat to low, cover partially, and simmer, stirring occasionally and adding water, if necessary, until the beans are very

tender, about 1 to 1½ hours. Take your time and let the beans barely bubble away until they smash easily on the side of the pan when pressed with a wooden spoon.

3.   Drain the beans and discard the bay leaves. Use immediately or cool the beans completely uncovered in the refrigerator. Store in small airtight container(s) in the refrigerator for up to 5 days or freeze for up to 3 months.

ACKNOWLEDGMENTS

Thank you to my editor, Jen Newens, for asking me to work with her again—what an honor. Thank you to my marvelous agent, Jenn Ferrari Adler, for her patience and dry wit. A big bowl of thanks also goes to Dina Avila for her astounding ability to make such beautiful images; Anne Parker for making the recipes herein look so utterly delicious; and Eric Fortier for his hard work in assisting and petting the pups.

A tip of my cap to the folks who inspired or donated recipes herein, including Chef Eric Silverstein of The Peached Tortilla in Austin, Texas; Leena Ezekiel of Thali Supper Club in Portland, Oregon; Mirna Attar of Ya Hala restaurant in Portland, Oregon; Alex and Shackai Jones; Chef Sompon Nabnian of Chiang Mai Thai Cookery School; and all the cooks I worked with at Pasqual's Cantina whose names I have sadly forgotten.

A giant dollop of guacamole-flavored gratitude goes to the lovely friends and colleagues who generously volunteered their time and taste buds to testing and helping me perfect the recipes in this book. Thank you to mole mama Cathie Schutz, veggie queen Jill Nussinow, vindaloo vixen Chani Olscn, luau lovely Cheryl Slocum, Tucson tenderloin expert Jackie Alpers, cheese champion Carol Penn Romine, Greek grill goddess Beth Richter Hatjopoulos, ceviche chief Ryan Smith, jackfruit jock Patty Wunder, fellow OS taco salad lover Sarah Hart, Sheboygan sweetie and Tajin pusher Michelle Smoody Nelson, fish aficionado Linda Cox Gilbert, Japanese yakitori-san Lauralee Garson, Packer family members Jim and Brenda Tiefelder, slow cooker pro Selena Darrow, Santa Fe chile sauce consultant Mary Wolff, Puerto Vallarta advisor Kristen Siefken, and duck dorks David and Susan Theis. Thank you for trusting me with your dinners.

And finally, thank you to my husband, Gregor, for his steadfast patience, and to my boys, Remy and Astor, for making me take lots of breaks for walkies.

INDEX

P

T

ABOUT THE AUTHOR

IVY MANNING is the Portland, Oregon-based author of ten cookbooks, including the best seller *Instant Pot Miracle 6 Ingredients or Less* and *Easy Soups from Scratch with Quick Breads to Match*. Her work has appeared in *Cooking Light*, *Bon Appetit*, *Clean Eating*, *Better Homes & Gardens*, *SpruceEats*, *Eater*, and *The Kitchn*. She is a regular contributor to lifestyle brands like Yummly, Fitbit, and Self. Visit her at ivymanning.com and Instagram @ivy_manning.